Performance Equation

The rocket science (Not!) behind how great
people, teams and organizations work

by Mario G. Patenaude

Copyright © 2013 by Mario G. Patenaude
First Edition –March 2013

ISBN
978-1-77097-431-9 (Hardcover)
978-1-77097-432-6 (Paperback)
978-1-77097-433-3 (eBook)

All rights reserved.

No part of this publication may be reproduced in any form, or by any means, electronic or mechanical, including photocopying, recording, or any information browsing, storage, or retrieval system, without permission in writing from the publisher.

Produced by:

FriesenPress
Suite 300 – 852 Fort Street
Victoria, BC, Canada V8W 1H8

www.friesenpress.com

Distributed to the trade by The Ingram Book Company

TABLE OF CONTENTS

About The Book .... *v*

Prologue *1*

The Concept *4*

The Foundation—Who We Are And Want To Become *8*

Business Strategy—Taking Bold Actions To Fulfil The Dream *19*

Governance Structure—How We Organize To Make Decisions *23*

Business Processes & Projects—What We Need To Get Things Done *40*

The High-Performance Team—Working Together To Achieve Common Goals *44*

Defining The Role *66*

The Right Stuff To Fit The Role *75*

Expectations For The Role *109*

What The Role Is Worth *111*

The Right Workshop *114*

The Talent System *116*

Performance Equation *210*

Conclusion—So What Does All Of This Mean? *232*

Epilogue *236*

Acknowledgements *238*

About The Author *239*

Bibliography *241*

To the members of the great Human Resources teams I have had the privilege of leading, the colleagues I have teamed up with, the team leaders who have guided and inspired me, and the subject-matter consultants who treated us as partners. Thank you for the learning and for your passionate belief in our people, our team and our vision.

ABOUT THE BOOK

The modern, and often global, organizations have all embarked, at one point or another, in the development and implementation of sophisticated and comprehensive people programs, which are designed to support their performance. They are now looking at simplifying their unwieldy programs. Conversely, the smaller or less advanced organizations are facing increasingly complex people issues, either because of the current environment or their need to compete, and are looking to upgrade their capability.

Both are converging towards the optimal middle ground; one wanting to become more sophisticated, the other wanted to simplify and streamline. The best organizations out there never really left the middle ground. They periodically upgrade their Human Resources (HR) program with the best-proven models and research available without sacrificing its integration or simplicity, but most importantly its outcome—organizational performance.

This book is about distilling down the complexity of leading-edge Human Resources and organizational performance concepts and models into their most fundamental elements, and show how each of them fits into a simple and integrated performance equation.

It is no longer a secret—nor a theory—that the performance of an organization is ultimately about the quality of its people, and how well they work together as teams to develop and implement the business strategies necessary to make them succeed in a global and increasingly competitive world. It is now a given assumption. The equation is mission critical.

The accountability for solving the performance equation rests with the community of HR leaders, team members and consultants who are the trusted 'people experts' the organization relies upon. But the daily application of the most important variables of that equation will always be the role of the team leader. The following pages may offer to team leaders and HR practitioners the thought-provoking ideas, as well as the necessary challenges to conventional wisdom and political correctness, needed to induce reflection and action on what the right HR program should be in order to solve and live the organizational performance equation. I hope it does.

PROLOGUE

Over the past three decades, I could not help but learn from the countless number of individuals who generously took the time to share with me their wisdom and knowledge of organizations, business and people and were patient enough to explain to me, in layman's terms, how it all really works.

I was fortunate enough to join large organizations that had the financial means and business imperatives to employ world-class business people and retain expert consultants. In most cases, the stakes and urgency of turning the business around meant spending whatever amount of money we needed to fix it quickly. I considered my colleagues, team members, and consultants as invaluable resources in my ongoing business education. I admired those who made complexity simple and fundamentally understood how their particular elements of business worked and how it interacted with others in a synergistic way. I despised—and soon came to dismiss—the notion that certain subjects were simply too complicated to explain.

As an HR leader, I had the opportunity to work for well-known and admired Canadian and global organizations, most of which are operating in industries focused on science, technology and engineering. Being surrounded by engineers and scientists (*Some of them actually were rocket scientists... and needed to be in order to understand the HR program*) forced me to take a very systematic, metrics driven, fundamental and integrated approach to doing HR. That is the only way I could convince my colleagues to support our HR team's ideas (*And its mere existence*). We could no longer be the proverbial 'mushy' socio-communists from HR or the mere overhead function needed to take care of labour relations and legal compliance.

I became an apostle of taking a scientific and engineering approach to organizational development and change management. This would take away the perceived unpredictable risks of dealing with people, teams and organizations away from the performance and change equations. I certainly did not invent or design anything new in the process. I simply integrated into what I call an 'integral' model what I learned from experts and case studies. I kind of became the 'Dell' of HR by simply integrating the best of available components.

It also became obvious to me that the combination of gaining experience in crisis management, communication and HR was going to be handy going forward. I was becoming a change-management guy.

What I came to understand only too well over the course of my career is that there were many constants and common denominators from an organizational performance and effectiveness standpoint, regardless of how unique a given organization or industry believed it was. There are HR principles and approaches that can be applied to any number of different businesses and industries. In the end, people are people, no matter what industry.

I wrote the table of contents for this book ten years ago, on a piece of hotel stationary. I suspect I was bored at whatever conference I was attending at the time. In the past decade I never had the time to sit down and write it. I was either too busy helping to turn around, merge or change a business, or in a freezing-cold arena coaching one of the boy's hockey teams. I finally decided to write this book on some idle and rainy Tuesday in December of last year, while contemplating what I was going to do with my professional life after having resigned my last position. My wife, who had decided to go back to work herself, teased me out of procrastination as a way—I suspect—of trying to focus my interest on something productive and valuable, instead of alphabetizing her spice rack or attempting to organize her large collection of shoes by style and colour (*How many shades of one colour can you handle...really*).

This book is simply about sharing what I have learned so far about how people, teams and organizations work. It is neither a research paper, nor is it an academic thesis or textbook with fancy graphics (*I did them myself*). It is a casual, candid narration about a clear, simple approach to having great teams of people working with great leaders and achieving great things together. I hope you enjoy the book and try applying the equation and that you will let me know what you think.

It works. You'll see.

THE CONCEPT

In any organization, the challenge for the HR team and its people leaders has always been to fundamentally understand the people factor, link it to the success of the organization, have the time to do all of the people things which HR insists on, and understand fundamentally how all of the people processes, policies and programs actually fit together.

In the scientific and engineering-driven businesses, filled with scientists, technologists and engineers, the typical touchy-feely language of HR never resonates well with the leadership complement and their team members. Most people in that world became scientists or engineers for a reason, being predisposed to enjoy or appreciate the certainty, predictability, and integration of their particular scientific or engineering discipline. They use mathematical formulas, a common lexicon, engineering models, blueprints, and anatomical charts. They need to fundamentally understand the system—human or otherwise—their subsystems, capabilities, and how they interact with one another.

Those of us who have had the benefit and privilege of working with such professionals, have quickly figured out that the only way to be successful in the people business, to gain credibility, or to make our job of developing them easier, is to align to their way of thinking and doing business. We are the outnumbered mushy HR practitioners who deal in the highly unpredictable and emotional world of people. The easiest people-related organizational element most employers understand is labour relations, for it is not emotional; it is the pure administration of a collective agreement. Most also understand academic qualifications and competencies. We strive to 'hardwire the soft stuff' into the business.

Of course, a big part of what we do is influenced by the business literature and conferences we attend. We shamelessly steal ideas and concepts from colleagues at industry seminars, and read about the latest theory or concept. I am a firm believer that there are several 'bibles' out there which have fundamentally altered or influenced business (*Buying business books at Costco or Target is a good start. They tend to only carry the business 'bibles' that sell above their prescribed threshold for a long period*).

That being said, repeatedly implementing the latest concept is a risky and distracting phenomenon, only supportive of a zigzag approach to organizational effectiveness. We all fear having to try the latest fad the CEO has read about in a magazine on a plane somewhere. That's why we use great consultants to help us figure it out, and tell us what has worked—or not worked—out there in the real world. They also help a lot in predicting if and how it would work in our own business at a point in time. We also ask them which new book they recently read, and which ones they would recommend *(Costco probably won't carry it for a while)*.

In the end, it's not so much which of the fundamental models or concepts is used, so long as one is used and integrated with the others. In other words, just pick one and apply it. Reputable consulting firms have tested the best models out there. They essentially all conclude the same thing, but use different terminology and semantics, or they got refined over time by someone else who did more research. Fundamental concepts and research do not have a shelf life. The idea is to continue to build on the foundation and further refine the models. That is what every scientific discipline has done since the beginning of time. Newton's law of gravity, for instance, still applies. New science just happens to offer better understanding, clarity or precision. Conversely, we should probably stop wasting our time and energy doing studies on some fundamental concepts and issues which we are now embedded in organizational culture (*We know that leadership and teamwork are key. Alright, alright, we got it!*).

TERMINOLOGY MATTERS

As members of a society where we can communicate in one of two official languages, we all know the importance of words, terminology, and their meaning. We learn from teachers and from reading and communicating with each other. In some cases, one single word or the concept it denotes can be the object of extraordinary interest and attention. For example, most organizations will proudly display the word 'respect' in their cultural statement, without considering the meaning of the word to you and me, let alone tens of thousands of colleagues from diverse societies and backgrounds throughout the world.

In the interpersonal communication world, how often do we argue because of having used a word with an intended meaning that did not get interpreted that way by a recipient? These words often trigger severe emotional responses. We also face the danger of inadvertently agreeing on an idea, thought, or principle that means two vastly different things to the two parties involved in the communication, only to find out later that we did not agree at all.

I also learned in the communication business that the use of particular words can conjure up some pretty intense emotions with people, or create images that are not productive. The use of a particular term can actually influence behaviours. For example, let's say your company has hired someone to dig around in your department and look for the cause of a certain shortcoming. If this initiative is worded as a departmental 'root canal', and you happen to be a person who is deathly afraid of needles and therefore dentistry, your reaction to this individual and the initiative as a whole will be immediately prejudiced. Consider the potential differences in perception between the phrases 'performance development' and 'performance assessment'. The former suggests a process that is constructive and aimed at helping people get better. The latter suggests a process that is judgemental and potentially critical.

In the technical world, be it engineering, medicine, law, or accounting, key terms are clearly and rigorously defined so that people are clear on what they mean. Even those of us who are not working in those fields now understand what a kilogram, vaccination, premeditation, or amortization means (*I think?*). And if not clear, agreed-upon definitions exist.

So let me define a few key terms we use a lot in the people business as we go through the book. That's what lawyers do in the front of contractual documents. I have arbitrarily picked the Merriam-Webster's dictionary (*Ironically, the word* ambiguous: *'capable of being understood in two or more possible senses or ways'—is on the top-ten list of most frequently looked up words on their web dictionary*).

THE FOUNDATION—WHO WE ARE AND WANT TO BECOME

In any organization, the foundation of all that there is to be achieved starts with who we are and what we do. It is what we dream of becoming and the values and beliefs which will guide us in making decisions on our way there. Only then can we figure out what we need to do to get there.

> *Foundation:* A basis (as a tenet, principle, or axiom) upon which something stands or is supported

MISSION & PURPOSE—WHAT WE ARE IN BUSINESS FOR

The organization's mission is where it all begins. Of course when you hear organizations and corporations talk about mission statements and purpose, vision and values you can't help but cringe. Way too much time is wasted in the corporate world arguing about the meaning of these words and where to begin. *(The only good thing about that is we had the meetings at some nice resort.)* The answer to that question is this: pick a set of definitions, and then start with the mission. It's pretty simple; we are either in the business of providing mobile telecommunications, or discovering pharmaceutical molecules, or whatever we do. That's what we are in business for.

Mission:	A pre-established and often self-imposed objective or purpose. Statement of the company's mission
Purpose:	Something set up as an object or end to be attained

Right there the dictionary is even offering another of the words we like to use—'purpose'. Well then, let's use both of the words and their definitions, and agree on a meaning, which is—the business we are in. The reason why it is important for an organization to know the business they are in is that it provides clarity, and a means of knowing when it purposely, or inadvertently, wanders off course. Also, it makes the one-minute elevator pitch to a guest or client about the business simpler to come up with for everyone.

A former professor of mine told us way back when that it was of paramount importance for us to know and agree on what businesses we would be in, as it would affect our perspective on the development of a business strategy and help us understand what we were passionate about and what our core competencies were. He used the Montreal Canadiens hockey team as an example. (*Being from Montreal, I am a genetic fan*). When he asked what business they were in, we all said professional sports. He replied, no, and said, "They are in the entertainment business." A good point, which explains why fans would stop going to the games or watching the broadcasts when goal scoring decreased, even if the Habs continued to win. Low-scoring games are simply less entertaining.

THE VISION—WHAT WE DREAM OF BECOMING

If the mission statement is where it all begins, the vision is really the dream where it all ends in the long term. Of course we go on to develop another vision, as we realize our dream. As most experts would agree, however, it is not advisable to modify or change the vision on a regular basis. It makes colleagues worry about how serious and thoughtful—even competent—the leadership team is.

Vision:	A thought, concept, or object formed by the imagination
Dream:	An experience of waking life having the characteristics of a dream: as a visionary creation of the imagination

The dream is the long-range destination, the beacon in a distance, the northern star. We don't know how we are going to get there yet, but at least we know what direction to head. We get rallied and mobilized around a common dream. Once that is done, we move to developing the business strategy to get us there. As Joel Barker, the individual who popularized the idea of paradigm shift in a corporate sense said, "Vision without action is merely a dream. Action without vision just passes the time. Vision with action can change the world."[1]

CULTURE, VALUES, & BELIEFS—WHAT GUIDES OUR DECISIONS AND BEHAVIOURS

The culture of an organization, which is the aggregate of its values and beliefs, is probably the most discussed and bantered about aspect of the people business. The reason for that is that culture and values are notions filled with not only vagueness, but also emotions. The culture or values of an organization define the way individuals within that organization conduct themselves in fulfilling their vision and achieving their strategic goals. For an individual, it defines what they emotionally value and believe in—how they live their life.

Culture:	The set of shared attitudes, values, goals, and practices that characterizes an institution or organization
Value:	Something (as a principle or quality) intrinsically valuable or desirable
Belief:	Something believed; a tenet or body of tenets held by a group

The senior leadership teams of organizations typically get together to develop the cultural or value statement, then test them with consultation or focus groups throughout the organization in an effort to socialize their proposal, seek input, and get buy-in from key opinion leaders. The output of those deliberations typically finds its way into posters and paraphernalia of various shapes and forms across the business. As we will see later, the output also finds its way back into the performance development and compensation systems as 'core competencies' applicable to every role in the organization.

It is impossible for a team of individuals to achieve high performance without each member of the team sharing in the same core organizational values. Needless to say, in a world where cross-functional and cross-national cooperation inevitably translates into greater performance and competitiveness, the core values of an organization must be common to all individuals throughout.

You are likely thinking right now—How can you have all colleagues value the same thing? That's impossible!

You would be shocked to know that global organizations actually develop cultural statements which apply to the entire entity, regardless of national boundaries or business units. What the organizations develop are the mission-critical values—or culture—they need to share in order to be successful. Of course, individuals and societies may espouse or promote many differing values, which is perfectly understandable and normal. Colleagues don't need to share all values, only the core ones.

The necessity to share in core or common values is not only related to organizations, but has been advocated by clerics and ancient philosophers as a means of achieving social harmony. Martin Seligman, the father of *Positive Psychology* and author of *Authentic Happiness*[2], found that six particular virtues, or values, were valued in almost every culture (Figure 1).

- Wisdom & Knowledge
- Courage
- Love & Humanity
- Justice
- Temperance
- Spirituality & Transcendence

FIGURE 1 — CORE VIRTUES

In any society or country where we recruit our talent from, there is a segment of the population who shares and believes in our chosen set of values. The key is to know where to find these people and get them in the organization. I will discuss talent acquisition planning in more detail later on.

Now you're thinking—So it's easier in certain societies or countries to find the talent that fits certain values?

I would argue that it is. Think of societies where corruption is institutionalized. It makes finding people with high integrity tough (*Probably have to bribe someone in the process as well*).

Organizations will expect that an individual's values and beliefs outside of the core values would be respected by colleagues, and actually valued for their diversity, for example, their political or religious beliefs. Religion and politics, of course, are all about values and beliefs, which are fraught with potential conflict. That's why our grandparents said we should never discuss them at family events; what supports family harmony are shared or core family values.

In the early days of so called value-driven organizations, we kind of realized that, for some strange reason, some of the most successful organizations in the world were, for the longest time, family businesses. That is because of a simple reason: for the first few generations of the business, all of the leaders were family members who grew up with the founders, either mom and dad or grandpa and grandma. The values of the family were, and became, the values of the business. Not coincidentally, those of us who worked for these family businesses saw why they indeed started to falter as the third generation of family members came on line and took leadership roles. They were not there with their parents or grandparents when they built the business, and didn't understand well, or believe in, which family values made the business so successful. They were also typically born in a much better financial situation than their grandparents, or even parents, and typically the 'nouveaux riches' are less driven to make it. They were also evidently born into a different generational cohort who, by definition, may have different value profiles.

What happens between generations, either in family businesses or simply in society at large, is now referred to as the generational gap, which is mainly a phenomenon created by the inability of certain individuals to evolve, adapt, and accept the particularities of the newer generation. The current leaders are Baby Boomers, ready to retire as a cohort, with the Generation X or 'Gen X' ready to take over. The problem of Gen X will be to deal with the next generation of so called Millennials. The Millennials believe that you work to live, not live to work and demand respect for work-life balance, which is not necessarily conducive to running a family business. They are innately sceptical, which translates into a strong need for authenticity, meaning integrity.

The ongoing challenge for organizations is hiring candidates from a pool of individuals who may have a different interpretation of the organization's values (*The multiple generation phenomenon is not new. Our grandparents said it about*

Elvis, and our parents about the Rolling Stones. Well...we say it about Lady Gaga. Just a different spot on the relative eccentricity spectrum – we have successfully raised the bar). While these cohorts of individuals may well believe in the organization's core values, they may also value other things which will impact upon their performance or commitment. The phenomenon supports the need for team leaders to understand each team member, recognize their needs, and accept the diversity they represent.

A few years ago, when the topic of generational gaps was becoming hot, I realized that the Fortune 100 companies and many of the top ranked 'Great Places to Work' organizations never really seem to worry too much about the issue. They are so focused on customizing the career experience to each individual colleague that the cohorts to which they belong does not really matter. Their HR strategy is designed for mass customization, and it accommodates individuality; furthermore, the team leaders know how to do it.

Most Fortune 100 corporations arrive at pretty much the same conclusion when it comes to the culture and values which they need to be successful (Figure 2). The number of values, terminology, and semantic may vary, but the essence is basically the same. There is something about a success culture which is almost universal. So, why do we waste the time to come up with the values if we all get to the same place anyway? The value in coming up with a strong cultural statement is the discussions, debates, and ultimately the buy-in of those involved. It is about leaders who, through the process, discover and agree on what the values mean and understand the behaviours attached to each value as descriptors.

- Customer Focus/Engagement
- Respect for People & Diversity
- Performing as a Team
- Leadership
- Innovation, Change & Continuous Improvement
- Honesty, Integrity & Commitment
- Creating Shareholder Value
- Social, Environmental, Community Responsibility/Investment

FIGURE 2 — TYPICAL VALUES FOUND
IN CULTURAL STATEMENTS

Just putting up nice posters doesn't work. In fact, if the organization is not going to live by what's on the posters, it is better off taking them down to avoid cynicism. These values and related behaviours have to be embedded into people policies and programs. They have to be monitored, measured, and enforced. These values will find their way into policies, practices and processes, pretty well as social values find their way into legislation. A corporation is like a tribe or a village.

The best organizations measure each individual's compliance to core values using the performance system, and will carry out 360-degree feedback assessments of its team leaders. They complement it by conducting enterprise-wide colleague engagement or value surveys every so many years to measure progress.

It takes courage and resolve for an organization and its leadership team to live and behave by these values. After all, they are saying that this culture is critical to the achievement of the business strategy and dream. The one value which most businesses do not compromise on is honesty and integrity (*Other than organized crime I suppose*). Failure to comply with that one is deemed to be cause for immediate dismissal.

Honesty:	The quality of being fair, truthful
Integrity:	The quality of being honest and fair
Dishonest:	Characterized by lack of truth, honesty, or trustworthiness

The problem with the term honesty is that it is often narrowly interpreted to describe an individual who does not engage in theft or blatant lies. That is why it is important to clearly define the behaviours which would be deemed to be in contravention of a value. For example, isn't it dishonest—and disrespectful—for a colleague to purposefully withhold information from another and wait for the right meeting in order to blind-side a colleague in front of the boss? If so, then should we not treat the individual with the same seriousness and severity as if they had stolen one of the laptops?

How about the word political? How many colleagues' names just came to mind as you read that word—Joe and Suzie? They're not dishonest; they are just political (*Yeah right!*). Did we not come up with great terminology to avoid having to deal with breaches of what we say are behaviours critical to our success? Making decisions based on political or self-interest information means taking action using erroneous or missing data (*Which is why integrity is so critical to success*).

Respect:	A feeling of admiring someone or something that is good, valuable, and important. A feeling or understanding that someone or something is important, serious, and should be treated in an appropriate way.
Politic(s)al:	Relating to the things people do to gain or keep power or an advantage within a group, or organization. Competition between competing interest groups or individuals for power and leadership. Political activities characterized by artful and often dishonest practices

We will see, when discussing the performance equation, that when team leaders claim that an individual does not fit in a team or organization, it is most likely to be at the cultural level. The misfit becomes evident, as it inevitably degenerates into what we typically refer to as a personality conflict, with all of the emotion and interpersonal drama, resulting from unacceptable behaviour. In fact, those heated conflicts should be more appropriately called 'value conflicts' (*Which is what wars are all about, aren't they?*).

BUSINESS STRATEGY—TAKING BOLD ACTIONS TO FULFIL THE DREAM

The development of the business strategy is where the 'rubber hits the road' *(Part of a Firestone Tire jingle in the '60s & '70s)* and the real test of the vision comes from. We typically set a few strategic goals to achieve on our way there, and then determine the actions required to achieve each of these goals.

One senior executive I worked for believed that a great game strategy should read: 'We must score more goals than they do.' He failed. In recent popular nomenclature, we also referred to these as Big Hairy Audacious Goals (BHAG's), as coined by Collins & Porras in their 1994 book *Built To Last*[3]. Can we really take the big actions necessary to move us closer to our dream within the long term? We used to develop five-year strategic plans and realized that business moves way too fast and unpredictably to continue to do that. We tend to use a rolling three-year horizon now.

Strategy:	The art of devising or employing plans or stratagems toward a goal. A careful plan or method for achieving a particular goal usually over a long period of time

The business strategy is really the first step in the regular and recurring business planning process (Figure 3). The strategic plan is reviewed in the earlier part of the fiscal year at a strategic planning/thinking session with the senior leadership team. The team essentially ensures that what we had seen over the three-year planning horizon the previous year has remained pretty consistent. If not, we have to update the plan.

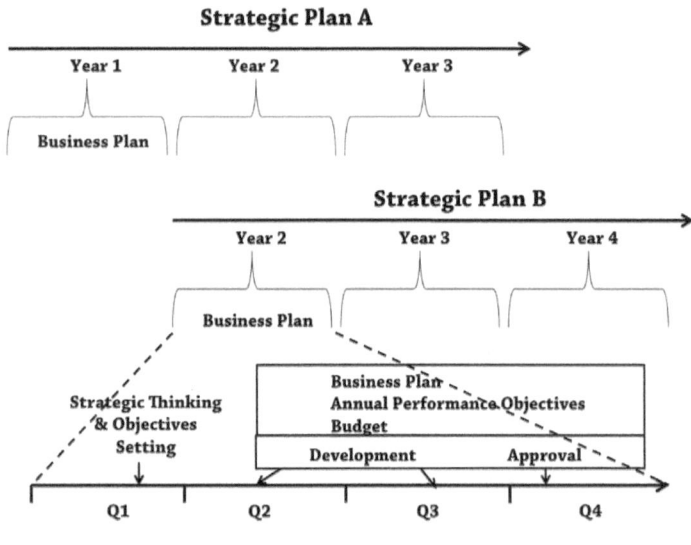

FIGURE 3 — BUSINESS PLANNING CYCLE

We then proceed at midyear to develop a detailed business plan for the following fiscal year (FY), which in fact is the detailed version of year one of the three-year strategic plan. This gives us time to prepare the budget associated with the business plan and develop preliminary yearly objectives for presentation and approval of the Board of Directors in the fall of that year. We can then start the new fiscal year with clear performance goals to support the achievement of the business plan and the associated budget and financials. Sales teams, by the way, love the idea of having sales targets and incentives ready for the new FY. How can you not have performance goals ready but have a budget already developed? What do you intend to do with the money? I will discuss the strategic goals later when covering the performance development system, goal setting, and compensation alignment.

PEOPLE & ORGANIZATIONAL EFFECTIVENESS STRATEGY—THE PEOPLE PART OF THE BUSINESS STRATEGY

During the process of developing or updating the business strategy, iterative conversations take place regarding the way the organization is structured, which business units we should add, the performance of teams and individuals and how to react to changing employment market conditions. The individual on the senior leadership team, or top team, who is accountable for people and organizational development and effectiveness, typically the Chief Human Resources Officer (CHRO), tends to lead those people and organization discussions. Of course, the CHRO is also a business person who actively contributes to other debates over operations, marketing, etc.

Once the business strategy is settled, the CHRO and their team are accountable for the development of people and the organizational development and effectiveness strategy, which will support its achievement, and which will further enhance the organization's performance. The strategy will typically be broken down by Key Accountability Area

(KAA) such as: recruitment, performance development, total rewards, workforce planning, employee or labour relations, organizational effectiveness and development, as well as operations. The key long-term or strategic-impact initiatives, such as policy, program and process changes and launches for each of the KAA, will be described, complete with project plans, budget and key performance indicators (KPIs). A major shift in business strategy would inevitably result in the modification of the organizational structure—structure follows strategy—and re-assignment of a significant number of individuals. The restructuring plan, like any other major strategic initiative, will be accompanied by a full-fledged change and risk-management strategy.

GOVERNANCE STRUCTURE—HOW WE ORGANIZE TO MAKE DECISIONS

In our discussions about how we organize to manage a business, we often use the term structure to fully define how we do so. Of course we know that decisions are not made simply within each functional or vertical silo (*We hate that word, don't we?*). We use leadership teams to do that. They meet on a regular basis to discuss and make decisions on issues and plans. We also have these committees to do the same on topics such as business technology investments and priorities. That is why we should call it governance structure vs. organizational structure. The organizational structure depicts the reporting relationship—who leads which team. The broader governance describes who—i.e. which stakeholder—and how we actually debate and make decisions and exercise managerial control. That includes the policies and processes.

Organization:	The way in which the different parts of something (such as a company) are arranged to form into a coherent unity or functioning whole. To arrange elements into a whole of interdependent parts

Structure:	The aggregate of elements of an entity in their relationships to each other
Governance:	The way that a city or company is controlled by the people who run it. To control, direct, or strongly influence the actions and conduct

Growing up in the business world, we all heard the expression, or dogma, which suggested 'strategy first, then structure'. Of course we kind of intuitively knew that all along, as we first need to figure out what we are here for—Mission—where we are trying to get to—Vision—how we will get there—Strategy & Culture—and finally how we should get organized to do that—Structure. All of which should be developed in that sequence. A Harvard professor of business history, Alfred Chandler, is the one who substantiated his 'Structure follows Strategy' thesis in the early 1960's based on four case studies of American conglomerates that dominated their industry from the 1920's onward. The structure is engineered to run the business and achieve its strategy. It logically goes without saying then, that restructuring in itself should not be a strategy. Restructuring should only be done to correct an identified flaw in the design, or support a shift in either corporate or functional strategy.

THE BOARD OF DIRECTORS

In any organizational entity, be it a family business, not-for-profit cause, or publicly-traded corporation, governance begins with a body we call a Board of Directors. The members are typically elected or appointed to the Board by the shareholders or members to represent their interests. The Board is sub-divided into committees whose respective mandates are to report and provide recommendations to the full Board on specific functional areas such as audit and finance, human resources, governance, and operations. The Board effectively keeps for itself the authorities it wants and delegates the others to the Chief Executive.

The link to the people or HR aspects of the organization is generally through a Committee, typically called Human Resources or Compensation. In some manufacturing or high-risk organizations, there is also an Occupational Health and Safety Committee. The Committees are charged with reviewing recommendations from management and recommends its approval—or not—to the Board of Directors. In recent years, Committees have availed themselves with independent advice from recognized and qualified subject-matter consultants. This is long overdue, as most members of these committees typically have no HR subject matter or functional expertise. Very few CHROs are Board members, which is a sad statement on how critical Boards consider having someone with HR functional expertise at the Board level is.

The effectiveness and appropriateness of executive compensation programs, as well as CEO selection and succession, which are three key responsibilities of the HR Committee, have been the object of severe criticism over the years, and rightfully so. The shareholders, and their lobby groups, argue that the decisions are not made in their best interest, and that they are made by Directors, who are also CEOs or senior executives of other corporations, and have a vested interest in perpetuating a self-serving status quo.

The worst-case scenario has to be the one where the bias is not only resulting from that phenomenon, but is severely aggravated by the presence of a controlling or majority shareholder whose financial ability to invest is the result of family genealogy, or cyclical economic luck. It is worth pointing out that being wealthy does not necessarily correlate to having management, leadership, or operational competency. In capitalist societies, we want to equate wealth with knowledge and competency, but that is not always the case. Not only is the controlling shareholder capable of naming disciples or bridge club partners to their board, they also further erode the already constrained freedom of speech and influence of Directors.

The case of the controlling shareholder being a private-equity firm can be equally damaging, for the primary investment motive is to make money quick or unlock value, rather than build something sustainable. This modus operandi is not unlike buying a damaged second-hand car for cheap, putting a new coat of paint on it, changing the tires, and installing a powerful sound system, then reselling it quick for more money than it's worth to a poor unsuspecting buyer. They make the numbers work for potential investors but not the people. Buyers are often not sophisticated enough to realize that the organization's people have been left weakened, disengaged, and ready to abandon ship.

Acquisition due-diligence checklists rarely contain executive team engagement, retention risks, or colleague-engagement data. Part of the reason for this is that most investment houses do not have resident HR subject matter experts; they will assign the human capital role to some partner with a personality, who probably has a business development background. Of course, not-so-clever investors are convinced that people will stick around to collect retention bonuses or to cash-in stock options. The investors too often project their moneymaking focus on a group of leaders who are passionate about the organization and its customers, and not necessarily money—they are not the mercenaries after all. Investment houses tend to forget that it is relatively easy for a savvy recruiting organization to eliminate the intended retention effect of stock options by simply replacing the individual's expected cash-in value of stock options with the equivalent cash value of options in its own stock.

INTACT TEAMS

The organizational structure itself begins at the top with a CEO, who determines which functions and leaders they consider to be critical to the achievement of the business strategy. Those functions are the strategic levers or controls of the cockpit from which the CEO pilots the organization. The CEO becomes the first team leader to integrate, consolidate, and lead a multitude of functions or business units. For example, depending on the strategy and industry, a CEO may want to integrate each of the traditional business-enabling functions himself (Figure 4) or delegate the integration of those functions to a direct report by creating a sub-function, typically called Corporate Services.

It's worth noting that modern depictions of structure are often inverted to illustrate that the CEO and their team are there to support the organization and its customer-facing, product making or service delivery individuals—in other words, the front liners.

- Operations
  - Manufacturing
  - Supply Chain
- Revenue Generation
  - Sales
  - Marketing
  - Product Development
- Customer Service
- Business Enabling (Or corporate services)
  - Finance
  - Human Resources
  - Business Technology
  - Communications/Stakeholder Relations
  - Legal

FIGURE 4 — TYPICAL FUNCTIONAL AREAS

The nature of these functions is strangely similar to a project's Work Breakdown Structure (WBS), which defines and groups a project's discrete work elements in a way that helps organize and define the total work scope of the project. That is what the first layer of an organization's structure generally is. The discrete elements are typically made up of a combination of functions and business units. If the business strategy calls for focus on a particular product area, customer segment or initiative, it is not unusual to have its leader reporting directly to the CEO.

Then the process of structuring the business cascades down from there, with each leader developing a structure. These units become sub-units within the organization and define at what level in the organization the functions are integrated or consolidated. Then each leader structures their team based on the function's strategy in such a way as to be supportive and aligned to the overall business strategy. The organizational structure begins to take shape both horizontally and vertically as interlocked intact teams are being formed, each of them led by a team leader (Figure 5). The CEO's team is often referred to as the top team, or Executive Leadership Team (XLT).

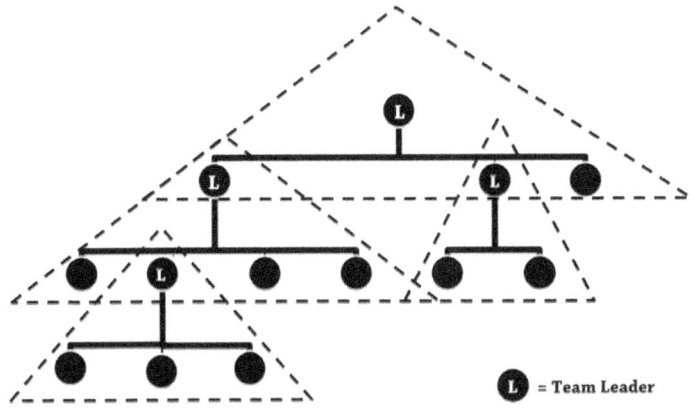

FIGURE 5 — HIERARCHY OF INTACT TEAMS

The individual held accountable for the integration of the unit's sub-units becomes the team leader. The last units to be developed are led by what are called first-line or front-line team leaders or supervisors, and they typically lead colleagues who are customer-facing, or product-making or service delivery.

Accountability: The quality or state of being accountable. An obligation or willingness to accept responsibility or to account for one's actions

The organizational sub-units, which are called business units, are typically designed around geography, product line, or customer segment and are responsible for the Profit & Loss (P&L) statement. It begins as a business unit, supported by partial or part-time functions, and then grows into being a self-contained entity. In most cases, those are embryonic future self-standing divisions, equipped with the same functions as the mother ship *(Though popular in science fiction, the term mother ship dates back to the 19th century whaling trade when small, fast ships were launched from the larger slower mother ship to hunt whales.)*

The infamous organizational structure chart, or orgchart, is then put together, typically by the HR or Organizational Effectiveness (OE) team, so people can visualize how they are organized. This often-underestimated key knowledge-management tool enables colleagues to better communicate with each other to access information—some would argue that Chief Financial Officers (CFO) love them just to monitor headcount.

The telephone book, either printed or electronically shared, has to be one of the most important and basic sources of knowledge in any organization, for it will point people to the source of knowledge. It can lead to chaos if not well managed and is not recommended in professional services firms, where the knowledge is best shared by having a well-structured and catalogued central repository. In large organizations, the book is typically structured in two ways: an alphabetical listing and an organizational one, complete with title, department/unit, email, phone number, and reporting relationship. The titles and levels are used as an indicator of what the incumbent's position mandate, or key accountabilities are. Of course, the ultimate solution is to have not only the orgchart but also every position profile accessible to each colleague in the organization, something which is a lot easier with today's technology. I will cover the position profile topic in detail later.

There is a strange phenomenon which often affects the published orgchart. In many cases, for some political or visual reason, the leadership of the organization or one team leader in particular, is reluctant to have one individual shown as reporting to another. So, the orgchart does not show the relationship. What that means is that a particular team leader actually exercises decision-making or leadership authority over an individual who is shown as reporting to another team leader. In other words, the 'real' orgchart is often different than the published one.

Authority: Power to influence or command thought, opinion, or behaviour. The power to give orders or make decisions. The power or right to direct or control someone or something

The orgchart depicts which team performs which function and who the team leader and members are. The individual's decision-making authorities are determined by what is in the position profile and should not be assumed based on reporting relationship. For example, the Director of Finance does not decide on all financial matters. Furthermore, the Director of Finance in one organization can have vastly different accountabilities and authorities than the Director of Finance in another.

In a highly performing and optimal world, each key business process is clearly defined and mapped out, complete with decision and/or consultation points in the process. Corporate governance policies dictate which level of decision-making authority the incumbent of each position has, either by hierarchical level or function. The most commonly known policy is the spending authority policy, which dictates how much the incumbent of a position can spend or contractually commit to, by type of expenditure.

LEADERSHIP FORUMS

There is a reasonable assumption in business that team leaders meet with their respective intact teams on a regular basis to effectively manage the business—Patrick Lencioni's *Death by Meeting*[4] is a book on the subject which is well worth reading. The frequency of the meetings tends to be directly related to the nature of the discussions being held. The weekly, monthly, quarterly, and annual team meetings are used for different purposes. The duration of the high-frequency weekly meetings is normally shorter and used for very operational and short-term purposes, while the annual one is the two to three-day strategy or business plan meeting. Those decision-making forums overlay on the organizational structure and exist by default.

While the intact team leadership forums are there by default, many other forums exist outside of the normal structure. These forums are either permanent or institutionalized or can be created for a period of time in the context of a particular initiative, project, or issue. The product development and business technology steering committees are two examples of institutional forums. The business development and executive committee meetings are also institutional meetings focusing on particular elements. The Enterprise

Resource Planning (ERP) system implementation committee is an example of a project-based temporary forum—I dislike and try to avoid the use of the word committee for it calls to mind the expression 'management by committee'. In both cases, either temporary or institutional, these forums are created when a team or project leader determines that it is not effective to have their entire team involved in a particular topic, or that members of other teams need to be involved in the discussions (*A good hockey analogy is the power-play line, which is made up of players from other regular lines*).

The organization should create the forums it needs to effectively and efficiently manage the business. That being said, the duly maligned expression 'management by committee' describes a decision-making process, which not only uses an excessive number of committees to consult/advise on topics, but also implies that a consensus of forum/committee members needs to be reached in order for a decision to be made. There are a couple of effective ways to depict such leadership forums (Figure 6).

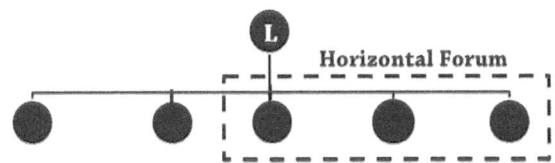

FIGURE 6 — HORIZONTAL LEADERSHIP FORUM

MATRIX STRUCTURES

It is not unusual in large project-driven or focused organizations, such as engineering and consulting firms, to have a large portion of the organization structured in a matrix. Ordinary businesses will typically only use this structural design for special projects or to deploy functional team members to other functions or business units. These functional resources are assigned to a project or unit, either temporarily, permanently, or on a part-time basis. They then become the object of a dual reporting relationship—to both the functional team leader and the project or business unit leader. The shared-services delivery or business partner model institutionalizes this reporting relationship, whereby a functional resource such as a finance or HR generalist is assigned to a business unit leader. In that case, all other functional services are provided from the mother ship.

In some instances, businesses will use multiple axes; for instance a business which considers function, project, geography, and industry might naturally subject colleagues to a four-axis matrix. The organizational community had to come up with another way to describe a secondary reporting relationship, other than the traditional solid line reporting relationship used in organizational charts. What it came up with was the dotted line. With the advent of in-house colour printers, we are now able to describe up to four distinct reporting relationships (*Talk about confusion!*). This is potentially the best example for individuals to inadvertently agree to two different understandings of the same word, in this case the meaning of 'dotted line'.

The solution to that potentially ineffective and conflictual relationship is to clearly define each of the reporting lines. That can best be done by clearly defining what accountabilities and authorities each of the reporting line leaders has in dealing with a team member—we will cover this later on. There is an easy way to describe the dual reporting, without investing in the clear definition of these accountabilities and authorities. The solid line can generally be defined as a leader's ability to dictate 'what' is to be accomplished, and with which priority. The dotted line authority for a team leader provides them with the authority to determine 'how' the work is to be accomplished.

It makes sense then that a member of a functional team, such as Business Technology (BT) for example, would take direction on how to technically carry out their work since their functional team leader would have subject-matter expertise in BT. The project leader on the other hand would have the solid line authority to dictate the scope of the work to be accomplished and by when. This means that, in fact, when a functional team member is assigned to a project or unit, the reporting relationship with his functional team leader, which encompassed both the 'what' and 'how'—or solid and dotted—now becomes a dotted one only (Figure 7).

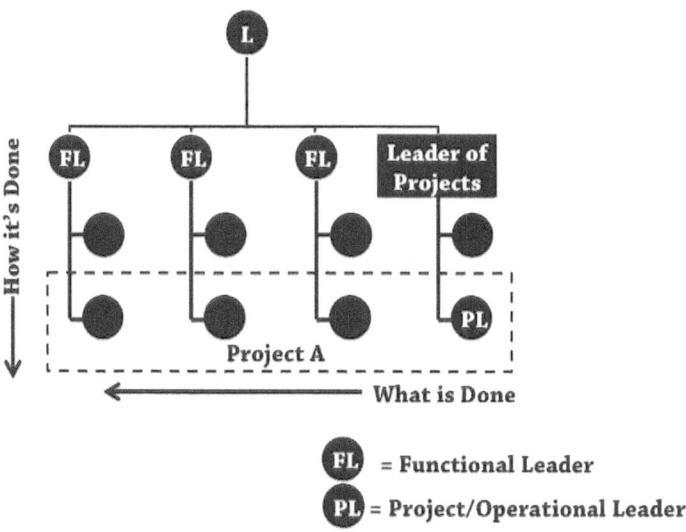

FIGURE 7 — DUAL/MATRIX REPORTING RELATIONSHIP

THE BUILDING CODE

There are a few simple rules which can be used when discussing or deciding how to design—or redesign as the case may be—an organizational structure. Of course, there are Subject-Matter Experts (SMEs), the effective architects and engineers of structural design, who get paid very well (*And rightfully so*). Nevertheless, the fundamentals of how to design and build a structure are important to know, for most organizations undertake the design themselves, unless it is deemed to be a complex exercise of gigantic proportions. Here are the simple rules.

Develop strategy first, then structure (*Of course...we already said that*).

Get the right levers. If strategy indeed comes first, then the next most critical step is to structure the organization—starting at the top—with each team leader having the right strategic levers available and their incumbents sitting around the leadership team's table when decisions are to be made.

Design your 'Ideal' structure, and then adjust for people and politics. It is inevitable that, in any structure, there will be exceptions or deviations made—either in transition or permanently—to accommodate particular people issues or address political sensitivities (*It always happens... that's just the way it is*).

Consider the next structural evolution. Unless lead by avid believers in the big-bang theory, most organizations consider it wiser to implement a new or 'end game' structure in phases over time. It goes without saying that each of the phased structures should connect to one another.

Ensure compatibility with the upper and subordinate structures. In cases where the structure is a component of a larger entity—such as in multinational or global organizations—it should be designed to connect to the upper or lower structure, as the case may be.

Design is as flat and wide as possible. The value of a flat, wide structure is that it broadens each leader's direct span of control, or how many levers are handled. It accelerates decision making, as there are fewer layers to involve in the decision. It also reduces the risk of the 'Chinese whispers' or 'telephone game' phenomenon wherein communication is slowed down and distorted by layers. The fewer the layers, the closer the people are to the action—either the customers or products.

Set the team to 5 to 12 members. This can be seen as the counterpoint to the flat, wide criterion above. The span of control should not become excessive, as it may result in insufficient leadership being provided to team members. The diversity and complexity of each sub-function—as well as the seniority or proficiency level of each of its leaders—will influence how wide the span can be. Expert wisdom tends to point to eight as the optimal team size, except in cases were coordination is minimal; the team can be fairly large.

Break job in two or re-assign components when workload is excessive. The instinct of many organizations is to assign additional individuals to a team in order to deal with workload issues. This creates many vertical one-on-one relationships. It is almost always best to break the job in two and assign a co-worker horizontally rather than a subordinated colleague.

A FEW DO'S & DON'TS TO REMEMBER

With great people in place, any structure will work (eventually). There is a recognition out there that, even if the structure is flawed, great people with effective leadership will work together to either fix it or will simply disregard it in the interest of getting things done well and quickly (*Of course it's better to come up with the right structure the first time.*)

The paper orgchart design is conceptual; reality can be very different. It's either that the structure is flawed or it had not been adjusted for people and political realities.

Refrain from using multicolour and multiple-reporting lines. If you find yourself having to do that, then you may want to reconsider the way you do business. Mass confusion, conflict, turf wars, and ball dropping—and therefore inefficiency—will inevitably be the result.

Use sports team analogies. The reason we use these analogies is that sports teams are simpler and smaller organizations to study and test our assumptions on. They have a limited number of positions and the Key Performance Indicators (KPIs) are simpler. In hockey, you are a forward, a defenseman or the goaltender. The leading KPIs include: shots on net, goal against average, penalty minutes, number of body checks, etc.

Don't just rely on titles. The use of titles alone forces people to make assumptions when it comes to accountabilities and authorities. Clarity comes with fully articulated definitions and communication throughout the organization. At a minimum, use the job mandate—why the job exists.

Restructuring does not fix performance. If you find that the organization is not performing, but that the strategy is sound, refrain from looking at restructuring as a solution in and of itself. It is not. Get at the root cause(s) of the problem(s). A Formula-1 analogy:

- You simply cannot redesign a vehicle during a pit stop
- Hard to race the car while being reassembled
- Very disruptive and costly
- Makes the driver worried
- Not necessarily the design – maybe needs a tune-up
- Problem could be the driver? The pit crew?

BUSINESS PROCESSES & PROJECTS—WHAT WE NEED TO GET THINGS DONE

It all started in early the 1900's with the era of Taylorism, Fordism, industrialization, and mass production—when business looked at better processes to efficiently produce their goods. Walter A. Shewhart, an American physicist, engineer, and statistician—now known as the father of statistical process control—was an influential author at the time. It was when Edwards Deming, (*Yep! He was an engineer also*) who ironically, as an American helping the Japanese automotive industry, pioneered Total Quality Management (TQM), the modern and enhanced process-based concept.

In the early '90s Michael Hammer—known as the father of Business Process Re-Engineering (BPR)—wrote his book *Reengineering the Corporation*[5]. *TIME* magazine named him one of America's 25 most influential individuals, while his book was ranked among the three most important business books of the past 20 years by *Forbes* magazine. Coincidentally, Hammer had a PhD in engineering from MIT, where he was also a professor. Motorola then came up with 'Six Sigma', popularized by GE's Jack Welch (*Not being a fan of the 'star CEO', I doubt very much if Jack all on his own made Six Sigma, or anything else for that matter, a success at GE)*. We then went on to 'lean manufacturing', brought to us by Toyota *(What is it with automobile people? Or is it that the Japanese just figured out the right way to build American inventions?)*.

All of these methods have their genesis in enhancing the output and quality of manufactured products while controlling costs. What is important to remember here is that the notion of process management evolved and will likely continue to do so. The original wisdom and concepts of the earlier 1900's should not be discarded as the next process concept emerges, unless it becomes totally obsolete. Some of its parts may remain an important part of how we get things done. We still teach Newton's Theory of Gravity in the age of String Theory.

There is also a great body of knowledge out there related to the management of business projects. In fact, processes and projects have a lot in common, and teams are typically responsible for both. One could argue that some processes are really reoccurring or continuous projects. In most organizations, the teams who are best at leading and managing projects and have the training and competencies to do so are typically the operations, manufacturing, or business technology folks. The building and construction team typically is good at it as well. Many of them even have formal Project Management Institute certification, called PMP for Project Management Professional *(I simply cannot understand why technical and business schools don't insist on having project and process management as a part of their core curriculum)*.

The understanding and mapping of all new and existing business processes—not simply the production and manufacturing ones—is the cornerstone of any business, for this is the only way to clearly understand and communicate how things get done. The people and technology are deployed to support those processes. Each team and its team members needs to know which task in the process—or project—is theirs to accomplish, and by when. The only way to reengineer or optimize a process is to understand what it is in the first place.

It is amazing that the process, or 'P' word, is often associated with slowness and bureaucracy by some. I like to use the analogy of a 17-person Formula-1 pit crew attempting to refuel and change tires in six to twelve seconds. Without a clear process, the right competencies and clear task accountabilities assigned to each team member, it just wouldn't happen. We too often forget that even discovery and innovation are actual processes. Granted, they require the right creative ideation environment, but they are processes nevertheless.

The challenge with these processes is that the critical enterprise-level ones are overlaid horizontally on an organizational structure that is defined by functions, which are understandably and rightfully designed vertically (Figure 8). In fact, the infamous process owner (*I don't like the term; it should be process manager*) is designated to ensure that the process itself is optimal, rather than make autocratic decisions about a process which crosses over multiple functions.

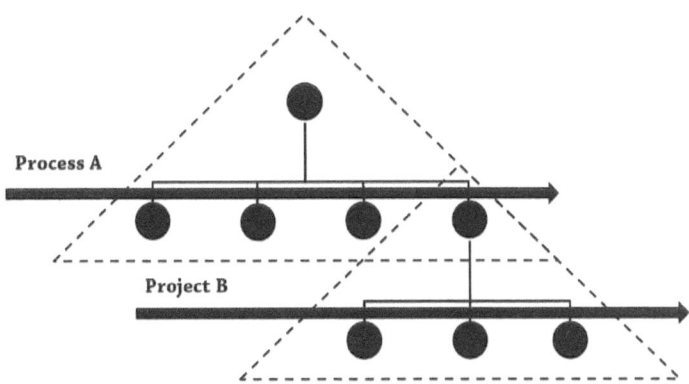

FIGURE 8 — BUSINESS PROCESS & STRUCTURE

It goes without saying that, if many other vertical functions are accountable for pieces of the horizontal process, the process manager cannot unilaterally decide on what the process is. A rule of thumb is that the individual who in the end 'decides' on the process is the individual accountable for all of the teams who have accountabilities related to that process. In the case of enterprise-level processes it is—or should be—the CEO that decides. The process manager has the right breadth of perspective, and hopefully competency, to decide on what optimal means and which trade-offs are best. Projects are very similar but are typically in a matrix-like structure; members of vertical functions are assigned to the project team and its leader (Figure 7). We will see later how role profiles, Key Accountability Areas (KAAs), and key accountabilities must clearly map out against each step into a business process or task within a project's work breakdown structure (WBS).

THE HIGH-PERFORMANCE TEAM—WORKING TOGETHER TO ACHIEVE COMMON GOALS

The next-level performance unit within any structure is the team unit. The top team, or Executive Leadership Team (XLT), is made up of the CEO and the leaders of each of the functions the CEO deemed necessary to steer in order to achieve the strategy. As we discussed earlier, the CEO decides which of these functions, or sub-functions, they want to integrate themself.

Team:	A number of persons associated together in work or activity
Teamwork:	Work done by several associates with each doing a part but all subordinating personal prominence to the efficiency of the whole

I never liked the clinical definition of a team. There is a much better composite one which means what we want it to mean.

A leader-engaged group of trustworthy, respectful, and mutually-accountable individuals with a requisite and mutually-understood set of complementary roles, competencies, and personalities, where each person subordinates their individual interests and opinions to the unity and efficiency of the team and creates synergy by making an inter-dependent and harmonized contribution towards the achievement of a common goal.

While the goal organizationally should be for each of these groups to evolve into high-performance teams, it is clear that, in the beginning, they are only groups of individuals. There is ample literature, research, and case studies supporting the notion that it is in the best interest of any organization to quickly have these individuals working well together or 'gel' to achieve common goals. One of the most recognized processes is Bruce Tuckman's forming, storming, norming, performing and adjourning model[6]. It is important to remember here that, while a group of disparate people needs a process to eventually become a team (*In sports we call that a system*) their actual performance will also be impacted by a few critical factors such as the quality of the team leader and the engagement level of team members. I will discuss those in the Performance Equation section.

The working-well-together aspect of team member relationships is what creates the synergy and therefore its enhanced output or performance. Aristotle philosophically coined the principle of synergy, a state of being wherein, "the whole is greater than the sum of its parts". The notion of teamwork finds itself into most corporate value statements for a good reason. The complementarity of competencies and personalities is also often reflected in values statements by using the term 'diversity'.

Business—and society in general—has now figured out that it is more effective and efficient to get things done with a team because of the synergy which is created (*We don't need a business case on that one anymore*). In the 1992 bestseller *The Wisdom of Teams*[7], Jon R. Katzenbach and Douglas K. Smith studied the critical elements of teams (Figure 9) and offered great insight into why teams work.

1. They Are Small
2. Members Possess Complimentary Skills
   a. Technical or functional expertise
   b. Problem-solving and decision-making skills
   c. Interpersonal skills
3. Members Share a Common Purpose & Performance Goals
4. Members Develop a Common Approach
5. Members Hold Themselves Mutually Accountable

FIGURE 9 — FIVE CHARACTERISTICS OF SUPERIOR TEAMS

In their 2008 book *Senior Leadership Teams*[8], Ruth Wageman *et al.* provided a slightly different perspective by proposing two sets of conditions supporting great teamwork—'essential' and 'enabling' conditions (Figure 10).

Essential:
- A Real Team: Bounded, stable, interdependent
- A Compelling Direction: Purpose-driven, challenging, clear
- The Right People: Conceptual thinkers with proven integrity

Enabling:
- Sound Structure: A small team with meaningful tasks and clear norms of conduct
- Supportive Context: Necessary skills for effective participation
- Expert Team Coaching: Not for individual members (for the team)

FIGURE 10 — CONDITIONS TO CREATE AN EFFECTIVE SENIOR LEADERSHIP TEAM

Patrick Lencioni, in his 2002 book *The Five Dysfunctions of a Team*[9], essentially agreed with the findings of Katzenbach but expressed them from the dysfunctional standpoint, i.e. why some teams don't work (Figure 11).

- Absence of Trust
- Fear of Conflict
- Lack of Commitment
- Avoidance of Accountability
- Inattention to Results

FIGURE 11 — THE FIVE DYSFUNCTIONS OF A TEAM

It is important to recognize that the vast majority of colleagues in the organization are part of a team, while others are both members of a team and leaders of another. The team an individual belongs to is a horizontal team, while the team they lead is known as the vertical team (Figure 12). Those individuals who perform their role, without relying on leading a vertical team are often referred to as a single contributor. I will admit here that I cannot stand the notion of first team put forward by Lencioni, which assumes that the horizontal team is the first team and the vertical team is the second team (*Or second-class team*). It is like asking a husband who his first family is—the one he grew up in, or the one he is now the father of. They are both his family, just different relationships.

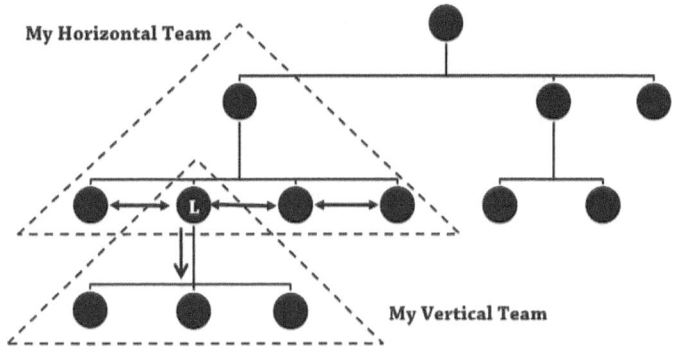

FIGURE 12 — VERTICAL & HORIZONTAL TEAMS

Some of the so-called technocrats (*Theoretical experts without practical experience*) of teamwork insist—and will argue—that there is a danger in overusing teams. That danger only exists when the entire team is asked to work on a task which requires only a particular subset of team members, for this is inefficient. A team leader demanding that a team carry out individual tasks, rather than common goals, is making ineffective use of their team.

While each team member has a role to play and individual tasks to accomplish, sub-performing individuals may also be tempted to delegate their own accountabilities to the team, thereby avoiding the risk and effort associated with the accountability. This diffusion of responsibility or 'social loafing' demands that someone else pick up the slack (*Probably where the term slacker came from, and probably related to not pulling on the rope. I'm just guessing*). Needless to say, that phenomenon generally occurs only for a limited amount of time, for other team members will eventually object and exert peer pressure in addressing this issue.

If it is indeed true that the synergy and output created by teamwork is paramount to the performance and effectiveness of an organization, and that each of the conditions necessary for teamwork to occur are variables of the equation, then teamwork needs to be nurtured and refreshed as any of the variables change. Teamwork should never be taken for granted once it has occurred.

The fundamental elements—or variables—needed in order for a team to gel and perform effectively are important to understand and recognize if we want to systematically operate as teams, and respect that core value of teamwork—a value critical to our success. These elements are:

TEAM LEADER

There is ample evidence that it is practically impossible for groups of individuals to develop into a team without a leader who is accountable and proactive. While we've heard of self-directed or self-managed teams, my experience is that there may be such a thing at the beginning, but a team leader typically emerges quickly, or different team members will assume the leader's role depending on issues and circumstances. The team leader is held accountable for both leading and managing the team—I will discuss the difference later.

DEFINED TEAM MEMBERSHIP

The membership of any team is determined by the team leader's decision as to which sub- function they need to have direct control over—who they need sitting around the table when debating plans and issues. The incumbents become part of the group of individuals that form up as a team and quickly begin to focus on the strategic goals for their function or project.

CLEAR ROLE DEFINITION

The role of each team member, while it can and will inevitably evolve over time, is clearly defined at any point in time. Later on, I will offer a simple and integrated framework and approach to clearly define any role. Let us use the sports analogy once more—picture a bunch of athletes rushing onto the court, field, or ice without knowing which position to play; it would be mayhem. Conversely though, you would not want players on the team who were unable or unwilling to jump in to 'cover' and momentarily assume another teammate's position should the need arise, for it is sometimes crucial to make quick adjustments if a plan does not work as drawn. In order for this to be possible, each member needs to know the roles of their teammates. This is covered below.

All of the experts would agree that team members must hold each other mutually accountable for their respective contributions. In fact, I would argue that by definition in organizations each individual is accountable for the fulfilment of their role. The role itself carries key accountabilities assigned to the role by the organization, and the team's leader. I would further argue that it is legitimate for team members to expect that each teammate will carry out their own role with diligence. The team leader is really accountable for ensuring that each of their team members is indeed fulfilling their role within the team. This occurs within the performance development process which will be covered specifically later (*As a terminology freak, I don't talk about performance 'management' as it is not here the intent of the program. Development is the intent.*)

Team members should hold each other mutually accountable only for what the team shares—the team's objectives, vision, and values. Holding each other accountable for each other's performance is a recipe for conflict and will usually result in the degradation of the team's performance. For this reason teammates can't criticize each other about the performance of their respective roles, unless the lack of performance of a colleague is preventing the other from performing their role.

If there is one fallacy which exists with regard to the workings of a team, it is the concept of the so-called 'team decision'. Teams, executive or not, don't actually decide anything. The team meeting is nothing more than an effective forum where topics are discussed, issues debated, and options tested in the presence of all team members, including the team leader. The team leader makes a decision once they have heard the candid debate and explored all alternatives on the full width of the spectrum. It is up to the team leader to decide if and when they will want to make a consensus decision, whereby all team members agree. The leader has the option of making either: consensus, compromise, majority, or autocratic decisions— hence 'situational leadership'.

MUTUAL KNOWLEDGE

One of the most impactful drivers of synergy in a team is the teammates' mutual knowledge of each other's personalities, roles, strengths and weaknesses. This enables each member to be predictive and proactive in their work, as they understand a colleague's reflexes and predict the next move.

Do any of these famous combinations ring a bell? Jordan, Pippen, and Rodman (Chicago Bulls); Bradshaw, Swann, Stallworth, Harris and Webster (Pittsburgh Steelers); how about Lafleur, Lemaire, and Shut (Montreal Canadiens). While these lines were composed of individually talented athletes, their strength lay in the athletes' knowledge of each other. Knowledge of one's team members also helps in communicating clearly while avoiding and effectively addressing misunderstandings. In turn, the mutual knowledge of roles and vertical team objectives allows for the minimization of what is referred to as 'gaps and overlaps' *(Which is to say ball dropping* and *toe stepping)*. These are often at the source of conflict between team members, who will get frustrated when a teammate inadvertently barges in on another's role or, even worse, is wrongly perceived as not fulfilling his own.

COMPLEMENTARY COMPETENCIES

Competent:	Having the necessary ability or skills. Able to do something well or well enough to meet a standard. Having requisite or adequate ability or qualities
Complement:	To complete or enhance by providing something additional. To complete something else or make it better

If a working team is by definition made up of individuals who are accountable for the performance of distinct subfunctions, it logically follows that their competencies would be complementary by default. While it is not uncommon for colleagues to have many shared competencies, a segment of their respective competencies is inevitably unique and complementary. The commonality of competencies is particularly useful in cases where a teammate has to step in to backup or cover for a colleague where workload or availability is an issue.

Of course the sports analogy works every time. In the NBA example above, while all these players played their respective and distinct positions on the court, they were each reputed for their complementary skills: Jordan was the greatest scorer in the game, a ball-thief and shot blocker; Pippen was the premier in your face defender; and Rodman was a tremendous rebounding specialist.

The complementarity of competencies is not as impactful in cases when a team leader is responsible for the leadership of several individuals who essentially perform the same function, e.g. a front-line team of eight electricians *(Call it a 'uni-functional' team)*. One could argue, however, that having incumbents with different technical or industry backgrounds—hence competencies—would be a definite asset to the team.

COMPLEMENTARY PERSONALITIES

Personality: The totality of an individual's behavioural and emotional characteristics. A set of distinctive traits and characteristics. The set of emotional qualities, ways of behaving, that makes a person different from other people

The diversity and complementarity of personalities is often an existing condition of effective teams. The distinct functions to be carried out as part of the team often require a certain personality or motivational profile. In order to achieve optimal operational performance, each team member needs to match or 'fit' the profile of their respective role, including its personality traits, at the reflex level.

For example, it is well recognized that the incumbent of a customer-facing role, such as sales or customer service, needs to have an extroverted personality. These individuals—contrary to popular belief—did not become extroverted by having to perform the role, but rather were attracted to the role because they were extroverts. Other common examples would be critical individuals who will ask all of the challenging questions, and the idea guys and gals who will want to discuss the big picture.

The concept of *Six Thinking Hats*[10], developed by Dr. Edward de Bono, forces teams into the parallel thinking required when debating a subject. In de Bono's model, extroverted emotional thinking would carry a red hat, while green hats would go to creative thinking, and black hats to critical thinking. The concept forces each team member to recognize different modes of thinking and their value and to be aware and flexible with regard to their own thinking style. In using the concept, it is interesting to observe that team members tend to wear a specific reflex colored hat based on their personality.

The diversity of roles to be performed by members of a team is therefore supportive of having multiple and complementary personalities represented on the team. Assuming that each personality is a match to the requirements of each of the roles, they should then be logically complementary. Individuals with different personalities tend to view issues (*And the whole world in general*) with a particular perspective. The diversity of these perspectives is critical to effective teams as it allows the team leader to openly discuss and manage output and issues with their team, with each member looking at it with a different perspective. This phenomenon is supportive of effective decision making, as the full spectrum (Figure 13) and all elements of the issue are likely to be discussed and debated before a decision is made by the team leader.

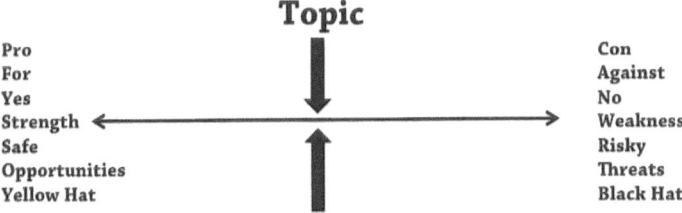

FIGURE 13 — TOPIC SPECTRUM

COMMON VALUES

We discussed organizational culture earlier and the need for each individual in the organization to share and fundamentally believe in its core values. If the organization is the macro version of a team, it then follows that each member of the micro version of it—the intact team—must share in the same values. In fact, as we discussed earlier, teamwork is typically one of the core values promoted by high-performance organizations. It is now widely recognized by SMEs on teamwork that mutual trust and respect are paramount to teamwork. I would put forward that, while respect is also on the list of typical core values, the underlying value which supports trust, has to be integrity. It is typically also on the list (*Not a coincidence*).

TEAM NORMS

It takes time for a team and its members to evolve into a full-fledged performing team, for teammates must discover and agree on how to work together or gel. The team needs to avoid making assumptions on how it will best work and needs to invest in clearly understanding and stating the team's norms. The notion of 'on-boarding' or integration is that process; it must be engineered—by design and not by default—for optimal gelling speed and strength. We often forget that, in any organization, team members, their roles, goals, and competencies are very fluid over time. A new team member failing to properly get on-board with either their vertical or horizontal team can have a disastrous impact on the team's performance.

CANDID COMMUNICATION & FEEDBACK

Communication: The act or process of using words, sounds, signs, or behaviours to express or exchange information or to express ideas, thoughts or feelings to someone else. A process by which information is exchanged between individuals through a common system of words, symbols, signs, or behaviour

Whether gelling or performing, team members need timely and accurate information—or data if you'd prefer. If teamwork is about working well together to achieve the team's goals, teammates need to learn, discuss, argue, and debate. That process is generally referred to as communication (*It is ironic that 'communication' is a term we commonly use and rarely understand well*).

Our misunderstanding and cavalier treatment of communication can have a seriously detrimental impact on a team's ability to gel and perform. Each individual's proficiency level with regards to the communication competency, either in a transmitting or receiving mode, is rarely considered. How many of us have actually taken effective communication training? There are several models out there which can be used in illustrating the risks and complexities of interpersonal communication (Figures 14 & 15).

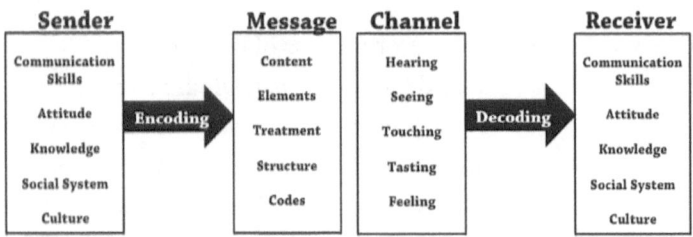

FIGURE 14 — BERLO'S LINEAR MODEL

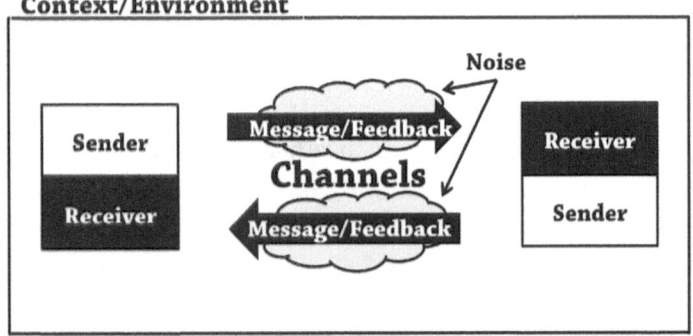

FIGURE 15 — BARNLUND'S TRANSACTIONAL MODEL

It is difficult enough to communicate effectively with one other person, let alone communicating in a team forum. How many inter-personal conflicts are triggered by the noise (Figure 16) amplifying the misunderstandings between teammates? The risk of misunderstanding can be effectively mitigated by individuals mutually trusting the intent of the communication—one more valuable effect of mutual trust—even when either miscommunicated or misinterpreted.

- Environmental
- Physiological Impairment
- Semantic
- Syntactical
- Organizational
- Cultural
- Psychological

FIGURE 16 — COMMUNICATION NOISE TYPES

That trusting of the intent can only be achieved when those communicating know each other well and have gained mutual trust (*How risky is it for a new person to join the team, but reside on another continent without having had the chance to bond or gel within the team?*). In the rush of daily performance, we now use this medium or channel called email, where the lack of two of the very critical elements required to effectively decode a message—hearing and seeing—prevents us from interpreting body language and voice intonation. Of course, when arguments and debates emerge via email, the repetitive exchanges and responses tend to compound the misunderstanding and therefore the risk of conflict. The instant messaging providers offer a tool to mitigate that counterproductive phenomenon by giving us the ability to add little facial expression symbols—smileys or emoticons—from a menu, in an attempt to add expression normally carried through voice intonation or body language. ☺

Feedback:	The transmission of evaluative or corrective information about an action, event, or process to the original or controlling source. Helpful information or criticism that is given to someone to say what can be done to improve a performance or product

The feedback element of any communication or action is paramount for the originator to gauge or assess the impact of the message they transmitted or the action having been taken as a result. Of course, in most organizations we adopted the term constructive feedback to promote the notion that unconstructive or destructive feedback is in fact a pseudonym for criticism, which most human beings dislike (*The vast majority of us are human beings. There may be aliens amongst us*). A former colleague of mine said to me years ago that, while the ability to provide feedback is probably one of the most impactful core competencies any organization can have, only very few of them do.

The ability to provide effective feedback or to communicate effectively is indeed a key core competency which each of us should have. Most of us are reluctant to provide feedback to a colleague or even a member of the team we lead for fear that the person will react negatively, either by being insulted or responding in a counterproductive way. If we believe that feedback is about getting better or learning, either as colleagues or teams, why would we not insist that it be given by culturally and systematically embedding the notion? Individuals should not simply feel as though they need to be asked or be invited to provide feedback, but rather should be expected to do so. The feedback provided should relate to the behaviour's impact on the individual's own performance and goals, as well as the organization's culture, rather than simply about how well the other colleague is doing his job. There are several feedback models out there which can be used *(Just pick one).* (Figure 17)

> **SIPP** - **S**incere, **I**ncident based,
> **P**ositive and **P**ersonal
> **W3** - **W**hat worked well, **W**hat did not, **W**hat can we do differently?
> **SLC** - **S**uccess, **L**earn, **C**hange
> **SSC** - **S**tart, **S**top, **C**ontinue

FIGURE 17 — FEEDBACK MODELS

My thoughts on feedback vs. criticism are probably best expressed by Daughtry and Casselman[11] *(These guys are Ph.Ds… I'm not)*:

> **Criticism** *is driven by the frustration and fears of the giver, not from the needs of the recipient. The underlying assumption is that the recipient somehow 'should know better' and needs to be set straight. The implied message is that the recipient's intentions are questionable, that there is something wrong with the recipient that the giver of criticism knows how to fix. In criticism, the problem is all in the recipient.*
>
> *In contrast,* **feedback** *has an air of caring concern, respect, and support. Far from being a sugar cookie, feedback is an honest, clear, adult-to-adult exchange about specific behaviors and the effects of those behaviors. The assumption is that both parties have positive intentions and that both parties want to be effective and to do what is right for the company*

and other people. Another assumption is that well-meaning people can have legitimate differences in perception. The person offering the feedback owns the feedback as being his reaction to the behavior of the other person. That is, the giver recognizes the fact that what is being offered is a perception, not absolute fact.

HORIZONTAL OBJECTIVES

By definition, a team is formed for the purpose of contributing synergistically to the achievement of goals which can only be achieved by the cross-functional, complementary and inter-dependent collaboration of team members. Horizontal objectives or goals *(Which I would argue are the same thing)* are those shared by each member of the team.

Conversely, the vertical objectives are those unique to each team member but shared one level down in the organization by the members of the team they each lead. Single contributors also have vertical objectives, which are different since they are not assigned to team members but fulfilled by the single contributor themselves.

EFFECTIVE DELEGATION

There is a pretty simple and fundamental assumption behind the concept of teamwork that we too often forget: having a team assumes that the coach lets their players play their respective roles. They don't get benched, and the coach does not get on the field or jump on the ice. So why are some team leaders reluctant, or incapable, of delegating authority to their team members, and will only delegate tasks *(They always have good reasons)?* (Figure 18).

- It is easier and quicker to do it myself rather than explain
- If you want it done right, you better do it yourself
- I can do the work better than anyone else
- If I am ultimately accountable, I am not delegating the authority

FIGURE 18 — MOST COMMON REASONS NOT TO DELEGATE

The role and challenge of a team leader fundamentally is to achieve objectives and run processes through the performance of others, while ultimately not abdicating the final accountability for their performance *(Now, that is a risky proposition)*. The delegation is of both the responsibility and the authority. The delegator never loses the accountability, but the delegate de facto becomes accountable and therefore cannot delegate the accountability either. Good governance says that accountability cannot be delegated; this prevents leaders from sidestepping the accountability and from being tempted to blame the delegate. Delegating tasks assumes that no authority is really necessary to be exercised. The delegation of authority, when you think about it, is a risky proposition, but it is critical to fostering both team performance and high colleague engagement.

The team leader needs to be capable of identifying and managing that risk, including taking corrective action if mistakes occur, which they inevitably will. The only question is this: is the potential delegate competent to exercise the authority, and can they be trusted to do so? Great leaders are good at such assessments, and also understand the importance of empowering their team members—the work gets done better and faster, and colleagues are engaged by their freedom to act—but don't blindly delegate. They use management and a control process to make sure that their judgement was solid and warranted. Great leaders will delegate more—or less—authority based on their assessment of a team member's proficiency levels and maturity.

The team leaders who struggle with the notion of delegation are typically those who cannot identify and manage—or in some cases tolerate—the risk and are too arrogant to accept the fact that others can be as good or better than they are, or want the credit and limelight for themselves. The inability to identify the risk is related to the leader's ability to determine a person's competency and judgement, which is often related to their personality. Introverts likely would have not experienced or sought constant interaction with people, and therefore would have a lesser ability to figure out people.

Introverted leaders often struggle with judging character, but are often effective at assessing tangible and technical competency. With experience and formal people-leadership models—including psychometrics—that issue goes away. Managing the risk is about having the right managerial and risk-management process and taking the right corrective action, which is, in turn, about the acquisition of managerial and process-management competencies.

Leaders who seek the political limelight and lack humility (*Or self-integrity*) should be deemed to contravene the organization's core values, which, at a minimum, should include integrity, respect for people, and teamwork, and they should be dealt with accordingly. Their behaviours will normally be identified through 360-degree feedback and organizational-level colleague-engagement surveys.

DEFINING THE ROLE

The position is the fundamental building block in any organization; it defines a cluster of accountabilities to be carried out in order to effectively run business processes or successfully complete projects.

The way the clusters are made up is very much influenced by the availability of candidates or potential incumbents on the employment market. That is because the competencies required to fulfil the set of accountabilities tend to be acquired in functional fashions out of academic institutions. For example, trade schools produce either a carpenter or an electrician, and never one that can do both.

Young accountants or engineers first become team leaders of other accountants and engineers before they become cross-functional leaders of other functions or projects—then they become the best customers of MBA schools. The position accountabilities begin to widen either within a function, or cross-functionally, with the CEO or business unit head being where all vertical functions within the unit become integrated by the team leader. Of course, the competency set required of a cross-functional team leader is broader than a functional one.

We generally define a team as a group of individuals, when we should really define a team as an amalgamation of positions, filled by presumably competent incumbents. What we mean is that the incumbent has what it takes, or the right stuff (*Which is what they said about the Mercury Seven astronauts*) to fulfil the accountabilities attached to the position, while respecting the core values of the organization.

We all know how passionate we can be when it comes to positions, for we all enjoyed participating in the annual budgeting sport and argued and debated with the finance team why we can justify adding a position or headcount (*I hate that word!*). The finance people also like to call them Full Time Equivalents (FTEs).

It took me a long time to figure out why people—and people in finance in particular—got so emotional about adding headcount. It's because it attracts overhead; the incumbent needs floor space, a computer, support staff, etc., and also comes with an employment severance liability. Being very careful about hiring additional colleagues also reduces the future risk of having to lay them off if workload diminishes. Adding resources is also often the easy way to avoid being creative and becoming more efficient. In short, it's a far bigger deal than just an additional salary (*I get it now*).

We often use the terms position and job interchangeably, but we shouldn't. The best way to describe the difference is to use the example of a sales team leader, which is a pretty standard job. However, two sales team leader positions can be very different, as they could be in different business units, geographies, with different reporting relationships and product areas. That job of a sales team leader belongs in its respective job family. These families are really driven by the standard vertical functions existing in most organizations. You may wonder why this has any relevance at all. Well, it is important to understand as it supports the concept of career planning and the notion that a lot of competencies found in these jobs are transferable to other jobs and even other job families. It makes the idea of talent planning much easier to understand and operationalize. I do not like the term succession planning, as it presupposes that we know who and when will take over for whom and are able to predict and manage the domino effect, which is a fallacy.

Once we understand what needs to be achieved within which values or culture and which business processes or projects we are going to run to get there, the next step is to figure out the positions and incumbents we need to do that. What I propose below is a simple and integrated way to define or profile a position. It is quite different from the traditional job description, as it focuses on the key accountabilities of a position, as opposed to all of the tasks which are expected to be completed by the incumbent *(I ask you, is it strictly necessary to have answers the phone when ringing added to each profile?)*. My argument and experience is that the development of these long documents was a bi-product of formal job evaluation point systems, which support the building of empires and use of key works to push the position's grade or salary up. In my opinion, they also foster a culture of, 'I won't do that because it's not in my job description or above my pay grade,' and the type of segregation of roles historically supported by trade unions.

MANDATE

The mandate of the position is really the mission statement for that particular role. It typically is developed during the budget season, when we start looking at funding and discuss why we need that position. The mandate should fit into one sentence.

REPORTING RELATIONSHIP

The reporting relationship defines to which position the position is accountable to. Where the position reports to is dictated by the team leader, based on where the other sub-functions or roles should or need to be integrated. If one were to break it down to its more fundamental elements, each position, and therefore its incumbent, has two distinct reporting relationships. The first one is the operational relationship or the solid line, which defines what is to be done. The second one is the functional relationship, or the dotted line, which defines how the work is to be done.

Those two distinct relationships are more evident in matrix or project organizations (Figure 7). In a purely functional one, the same individual is accountable for both the operational and functional relationships. In more complex structures, where the matrix includes geography and industry, for example, a few specific accountabilities are removed from the functional leader, and assigned to a regional or industry sector lead. Some organizations, such as consulting firms, decided early on to segregate the career development accountabilities and assigned them to either internal or external career coaches, mentors or managers. It is becoming more popular now that we understand that it is very challenging, and somewhat conflicting, for team leaders to also be effective career coaches.

ACCOUNTABILITIES & AUTHORITIES (As & As)

I was first exposed in the late '80s to the concept of science-based organizational development when I worked in the space business (*Our CEO was an engineer...of course*). I had the opportunity to work with renowned Canadian psychoanalyst and organizational psychologist Elliot Jaques, the author of *Requisite Organization*[12] who had developed a simple way to define role authorities and accountabilities. Jaques was not only an author; he was also a consultant to industry and government (*And is the one who coined the notion of 'mid-life crisis'*).

Other components of his research were used to structure organizations, identify potential, and select future leaders. His way of defining authorities—some people call them decision rights—is fundamentally simple and critical in clearly defining roles. It essentially defines who has which authority to do what in the team or unit (Figure 19). His approach was criticized for being very scientific and rigid, but one does not have to buy all of the components of his concept or life-time research, merely take the pieces which are helpful in making things better, clearer, and simpler. You don't have to pick this model; pick one which helps in defining who is accountable for what, and has which level of authority.

- To decide
- To recommend
- To veto
- To stop/delay process
- To audit/verify
- To consult
- To be consulted
- To inform
- To be informed

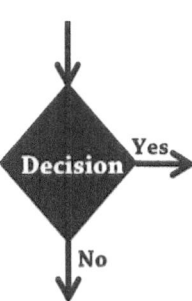

*Adapted from Requisite Organization

FIGURE 19 — REQUISITE AUTHORITY
LEVELS (OR DECISION RIGHTS)

Although less precise, the RACI (Figure 20) responsibility-assignment matrix model is another way to do the same and is popular in the sphere of project management.

> **R**esponsible
> **A**ccountable
> **C**onsulted
> **I**nformed

FIGURE 20 — RACI AUTHORITY LEVELS

The 'to do what' part of the equation—also known as Key Accountability Area (KAA)—is really the various steps or elements of each business process or project, such as selling, purchasing or recruiting, for which a role is accountable. If one were to take the map of each business process and artificially paste each of the relevant steps of the process map on a sheet of paper called role profile under the key accountabilities section, this would become the role's key accountabilities (Figure 21). The same would work by mapping out each element of a project plan.

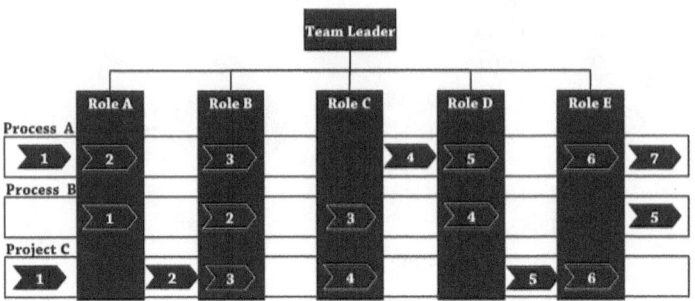

FIGURE 21 — ASSIGNMENT OF PROCESS
ACCOUNTABILITIES TO ROLES

The concept of shared accountability for a process step is a recipe for confusion and conflict. Of course, for each business process, many roles have accountabilities for the totality of the steps mapped out for the process. But it is important that each step in the process be assigned to a particular role, and only one. The only thing that is shared is the process itself, as several roles make up for the total accountabilities for the entire process. As we discussed earlier, the process manager is accountable to ensure that the process is defined, effective, and efficient, and that the totality of the process steps have been assigned to various roles within or outside of any one team.

The concept of accountability is neither new nor complex in itself, but is probably the cornerstone of any organization. It ensures that business processes and projects are run smoothly. It is a simple tool to clearly identify who is accountable on the team for which step in the process. A few important fundamental principles need to be respected:

- Accountability cannot be sidestepped. The team leader is accountable for the actions of their team members.

The CEO is ultimately accountable for all teams and their actions and cannot divest themselves from wrongdoing. The person who gets fired or reprimanded is the person along the chain of actions who is guilty of a wilful act or negligence (*A colleague of mine used to refer to the leadership style of certain individuals as the 'Ole!' style of leadership, equating a team leader side-stepping accountability with a matador side-stepping the bull, with the unsuspecting team member suddenly being ploughed over after the red sheet has been lifted*).

- As & As continually get refined, so it is important for team leaders and members to be vigilant, particularly when business processes and projects are modified, or roles within the team are modified, created, or eliminated.
- No one individual can either have or exercise a 'decide' authority on matters which substantially affect others outside of their vertical team. This means, for example, that the facilities manager cannot decide on the building's ambient temperature; the site manager does. The facilities manager recommends the temperature.
- An accountability cannot be assigned without the authority and resources necessary to fulfil it. We all have heard the expression, and felt the frustration which goes along with it. In most cases the authority is right, but the accountability is ill-stated or misunderstood.

STANDARD POSITION TEMPLATES

The roles of team leader, project manager, and single contributor—regardless of which functional area they are part of—are essentially standard roles which can be easily defined. As we discussed earlier, these three roles can simply be considered as fundamental jobs. The organization will benefit from developing what it sees as the ideal role for the leader of any team or project to play; it will then use it as a template for all such roles. As an example, any functional team leader should be accountable for the development of members of their team and should therefore have the corresponding team leadership and managerial competencies. Project managers should not be accountable for team member development.

THE RIGHT STUFF TO FIT THE ROLE

There is a set of elements contained in the role profile which the incumbent must fit in order for the role to be performed to its optimal level. Three of these elements: personality, intellect and values are innate to the incumbent and can rarely be changed, unless triggered by a significant life-altering emotional event or prolonged therapy, which organizations are not in the business of managing. That being said, individuals learn to suppress counterproductive behaviours which are either anchored in personality or values. Those behaviours, however, rapidly come to the surface upon applying stress, pressure, or fatigue which explains spikes of inappropriate behaviours for some individuals in those circumstances (*Intoxicants have a similar effect. People may say that Uncle Joe is not himself when he drinks. Well… he actually is himself!*). The great benefit of understanding the fundamental or reflex personality and values of an individual is that they are both stress resistant—or perhaps you could say stress transparent.

COMPETENCIES

Each of us has said, at one time or another, that a certain colleague is competent or not, meaning that the person could do the job well or not. The risk of using such a general statement and concept is that it does not allow for a simple and predictive way to understand why a person is indeed competent or not—or if they will be in another role. Competency is about breaking down a role into its fundamentally required abilities, behaviour, skills, or knowledge to be performed, and at what proficiency level.

An article by David C. McClelland entitled *Testing for Competence Rather Than for Intelligence*[13], published in 1973 made him widely recognized as the father of the competency movement. He argued that intelligence or IQ was probably not the best predictor of performance in a role. McClelland is the founder of the McBer and Company consultancy, where Richard Boyatzis—who became its CEO in 1976—authored *The Competent Manager*[14] in 1982. Boyatzis, who holds a BS in Aerodynamics and astronautics from MIT and a Ph.D. in Social Psychology from Harvard, is credited for having popularized the concept of competency. The consulting firm was later acquired by the Hay Group, which is well known for its job evaluation methodology and now has one of the best competency-management methodologies around.

The gurus of competency management were successful in breaking down role competence in a dictionary of the fundamental behavioural competencies required to perform any role known to human kind. Some of these competency dictionaries can contain up to 30 distinct competencies. The original McBer dictionary contained 18 (Figure 22).

1. Achievement Orientation
2. Analytical Thinking
3. Conceptual Thinking
4. Customer Service Orientation
5. **Developing Others**
6. Directiveness
7. Flexibility
8. Impact and Influence
9. Information Seeking
10. Initiative
11. Integrity
12. Interpersonal Understanding
13. Organizational Awareness
14. Organizational Commitment
15. Relationship Building
16. Self Confidence
17. Team Leadership
18. Teamwork and Cooperation

FIGURE 22 — ORIGINAL MCBER COMPETENCY DICTIONARY

The dictionaries typically include the description of each of the competencies, and specific descriptors for each of the 5 or 6 proficiency levels, as the McBer Scaled Competency Dictionary does (Figure 23). They can be purchased from leading consulting firms, who also offer role profiling, training, and model development and installation services. The Lominger *Leadership Architect*® suite, for example, contains 67 competencies, 19 career stallers and stoppers, and seven global focus areas.

Developing Others: Involves a genuine intent to foster the long-term learning or development of others with an appropriate level of need analysis and other thought or effort. Its focus is on the developmental intent and effect rather than on a formal role of training.

Proficiency Level	This Person:
1	**Expresses Positive Expectations of Person:** Makes positive comments regarding others' developmental future: current and expected future abilities and/or potential to learn even in "difficult" cases. Believes others want to and can learn or improve their performance.
2	**Gives How-to Directions:** Gives detailed instructions and/or on-the-job demonstrations, tells how to do the task, makes specific, helpful suggestions.
3	**Gives Reasons, Other Support:** Gives directions or demonstrations with reasons or rationale as a training strategy. Gives practical support or assistance to make job easier for subordinate (i.e., volunteers additional resources, tools, information, expert advice, etc.). Asks questions, gives tests, or uses other methods to verify that others have understood explanation or directions.
4	**Gives Feedback to Encourage:** Gives specific positive or mixed feedback for developmental purposes. Reassures others after a setback. Gives negative feedback in behavioral rather than personal terms, and expresses positive expectations for future performance or gives individualized suggestions for improvement
5	**Does Longer-term Coaching or Training:** Arranges appropriate and helpful assignments, formal training, or other experiences for the purpose of fostering a person's learning and development. Has people work out answers to problems themselves so they really knowhow, rather than simply giving them the answer. This does not include formal training done simply to meet corporate requirements. May include identifying a training or developmental need and establishing new programs or materials to meet it.

FIGURE 23 — PROFICIENCY LEVEL DESCRIPTORS – 'DEVELOPING OTHERS' COMPETENCY

The proficiency levels can also be simply described by using a generic scale (Figure 24)

>Level 1 = Awareness
>Level 2 = Basic
>Level 3 = Intermediate
>Level 4 = Advanced
>Level 5 = Expert

FIGURE 24 — GENERIC PROFICIENCY LEVELS

Some organizations elect to develop their own custom model and dictionary. NASA, for example, has a comprehensive dictionary with hundreds of behavioural and technical competencies, broken down in 5 distinct domains, clusters or families: Business, Engineering & Technology, Mission Operations, Leadership & Management, and Science (*I don't suggest that as the standard. They are, after all, rocket scientists*).

Organizations will further refine their use of competencies by developing a competency model or framework which describes which type of competencies are required to be effective in a particular role. The model will break down the competencies required by leaders, those required by specific families of roles or functions, those professional or technical competencies required in certain roles, and finally, those competencies required by all and any role (Figure 25). The leadership competencies are typically strategy driven, while the core competencies are derived from the organization's culture, or values.

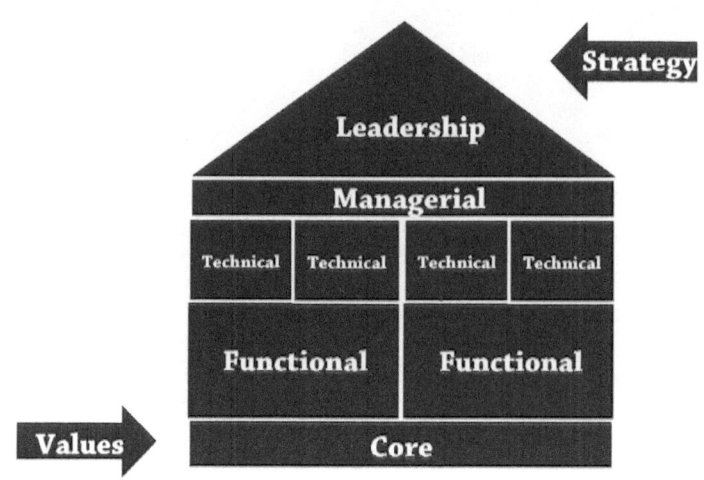

FIGURE 25 — COMPETENCY MODEL ARCHITECTURE

For example, a sales role requires the ability to put a proposal together, which can be called a technical competency (*I stayed away from using the example of expense-account preparation, which sales people notoriously attempt to either delegate or eliminate...*). The same competency can be called a family or functional one if it were to apply to each role in the revenue-generation family. The fundamental differences between these competencies are important, as they become useful in the recruiting and selection process, either internally or externally, as well as the development of incumbents in their current role or in preparation of a future one identified in their career development plan.

People naturally enhance their proficiency in a particular competency area, or acquire new competencies just by working and living. They do that within organizations for sure. So what do schools do? They provide knowledge transfer to their students, who in turn will apply it and turn it into actual competencies.

One of my favourite illustrations of that phenomenon is the use of the automotive engineering family of roles, using the automobile as a case study object. The first level of proficiency for someone entering at the bottom of the proficiency scale would be to have the knowledge to identify an automobile and its sub systems, such as engine, suspension, transmission, etc. Someone with that proficiency level could potentially perform the role of a detailer at a car dealership. However, they would need learning, either formal or On-the-Job-Training (OJT), to effectively acquire the competencies to perform the role. This would transform knowledge into competency at a certain proficiency level.

An automotive mechanic could have gone to trade or vocational school to perform the next role in the family. The individual would know how to take an engine apart and rebuild it, but could not actually do it without performing the task at least once. It is reasonable to assume that the individual's proficiency and performance would increase with the frequency of having performed the task. You can well imagine why formal education, rather than trial and error, would make that process faster. The frequency and repetition of the task is what we refer to as experience.

Experience is only an assumption of proficiency enhancement and competency acquisition. That assumption can only be verified by repeatedly observing its tangible demonstration, or through practical or role-playing testing. Some individuals learn, acquire competencies, or enhance proficiency significantly faster than others (*Particularly high-potentials*). The quality of the experience, formal training, and developmental coaching/mentoring are also factors which speed up competency acquisition, proficiency enhancement, and ultimately role performance.

The next level in the family would be the technician, who can diagnose issues and recommend courses of action for the mechanic to implement. The engineering level would be where vehicle systems are designed. The Professor of automotive engineering (*If there is such a thing*) would be the Level-5 or expert in the job family (Figure 26).

Level	Job	Proficiency
1	Detailer	Awareness
2	Mechanic	Basic
3	Technician	Intermediate
4	Engineer	Advanced
5	Professor	Expert

FIGURE 26 — AUTOMOTIVE ENGINEERING JOB FAMILY

Core

Core: A central and often foundational part usually distinct from the enveloping part by a difference in nature. A basic, essential, or enduring part

This set of competencies is directly related to the culture or values promoted by the organization. As we discussed earlier, the sharing of core values—and hence competencies—is a prerequisite to teamwork and team effectiveness. Each of the organization's core values needs to find its way in every position profile throughout the organization as a core competency, complete with behaviour description and proficiency level descriptors, as illustrated above.

The meaning of the organization's culture, or success values, becomes real in the daily organizational life through clearly explaining what is meant by each of the values and what behaviours are expected. The core competency of teamwork—which is always a core competency—for example, could be defined this way:

> Works collaboratively with colleagues to achieve team goals; Solicits input by genuinely valuing others' ideas and expertise; is willing to learn from and teach others; Places team priorities before personal agenda; Supports and acts in accordance with the team's decisions, even when not exactly reflecting their own position; Shares credit for team accomplishments and accountability for team shortcomings

Leadership

We used to ask ourselves the question: 'Are leaders born or made?' Then we attempted to differentiate leadership from management. Personally I'm not sure if we ever answered the question or if it really mattered anyway. Whether made or born, in organizations, what matters are the behaviours and outcomes of leadership. It so happens that some individuals' personalities or personal values may make the path to becoming a great leader easier for them. The more natural leadership is, the less energy it takes the incumbent to be one. What we were also seeing was the evolution of the manager into a team leader, with leader being more people focused, participative and influence vs. authority powered; this evolution was probably made necessary by significant environmental changes in the organization, such as the arrival of new generations of colleagues (*The dinosaurs weren't so lucky*).

Leader:	A person who has commanding authority or influence. Someone who guides other people

The best leaders I have met had the courage to state reality, the credibility and ability to inspire or engage people into believing in a vision, which at first seemed too ambitious. They gave them the self-confidence to invest their passion, determination, and energy in finding a way to get there, accompanied them during the journey, and finally praised and thanked their team for an extraordinary achievement. A great leader credits the team for the win and takes the blame for the loss. The emotional energy which fuels a team subjected to great leadership is far more potent than the application of authority or fear-based leadership and its inherent aseptic nature.

It would be a mistake to assume that leadership only belongs to those who are accountable for others, or a team. In some organizations, leadership is stated as a core value, with its behaviours expected of all colleagues, regardless of their role. It is also a means of identifying and developing future team leaders very early on.

There is, nevertheless, value in looking at the competencies of both leaders and managers, if it is only for the purpose of reminding ourselves that neither set of competencies are effective without the other. The competencies associated with leadership are often developed by organizations through the use of a competency dictionary and consulting help, though sometimes it is purely developed by coming up with indigenous behaviour statements. They essentially define which leadership competencies, and at which proficiency level they believe every leader needs to have in order to achieve the business strategy, within the confines of the organization's culture. The proficiency level is typically matched to each hierarchic level.

Most popular leadership competency models tend to break leadership competencies in three distinct clusters, such as the one used by the Center for Creative Leadership (CCL) (Figure 27).

Leading the Business	Leading Others	Leading Self/by Personal Example
Sound Judgment	Inspiring Commitment	Courage
Strategic Planning	Forging Synergy	Executive Image
Leading Change	Developing and Empowering	Learning from Experience
Results Orientation	Leveraging Differences	Credibility
Global Awareness	Communicating Effectively	
Business Perspective	Interpersonal Savvy	

FIGURE 27 — CLUSTERED LEADERSHIP COMPETENCY MODEL

Another view of leadership competencies, offered by Collins in his *Good to Great*[15] bestseller, describes the developmental progression individuals tend to follow in achieving the ultimate Level-5 Leadership (Figure 28) required to take organizations or teams from being good to being great (*The book should have be entitled 'From good enough to great'*). I had the privilege to work with a great leadership development consultant, who had helped build the Bombardier conglomerate and who used to consider humility as a fundamental element of leadership. He referred to humility as self-integrity (*It begs the question: should we consider those who lack humility, or are arrogant, as being dishonest?*).

Arrogance: An attitude of superiority manifested in an overbearing manner or in presumptuous claims or assumptions. An insulting way of thinking or behaving that comes from believing that you are better, smarter, or more important than other people

Level	Descriptor	Behavior
1	Highly-capable individual	Makes productive contributions through talent, knowledge, skills and good work habits
2	Contributing team member	Contributes to the achievement of group objectives; works effectively with others in a group setting
3	Competent manager	Organizes people and resources toward the effective and efficient pursuit of pre-determined objectives
4	Effective leader	Catalyzes commitment to and vigorous pursuit of a clear and compelling vision; stimulates the group to high-performance standards
5	Executive	Builds enduring greatness through a paradoxical combination of personal humility plus professional will

FIGURE 28 — LEVEL-5 LEADERSHIP PROGRESSION

Robert K. Greenleaf launched the modern servant leadership movement in his 1970 essay, *The Servant as Leader*[16] in which he coined the terms servant-leader and servant leadership. Larry Spears, who served for seventeen years as the head of the Greenleaf Center for Servant Leadership, identified ten characteristics of the servant leader (Figure 29).

- Listening
- Empathy
- Healing
- Awareness
- Persuasion
- Conceptualization
- Foresight
- Stewardship
- Commitment to the Growth of Others
- Building Community

FIGURE 29 — GREENLEAF'S SERVANT LEADER CHARACTERISTICS

Ken Blanchard and Paul Hersey, in their 1972 book *Management of Organizational Behavior*[17] put forward another view of leadership, which called for a leader to have the ability or competency to adopt differing leadership styles (Figure 30) based on the maturity of their team and members. They called it Situational Leadership.

- Telling/Directing
- Selling/Coaching
- Participating/Supporting
- Delegating/Observing

FIGURE 30 — SITUATIONAL LEADERSHIP STYLES

In the book *Primal Leadership*[18], Daniel Goleman, who popularized the notion of Emotional Intelligence, describes six different styles of leadership (Figure 31). The most effective leaders can move among these styles, adopting the one that meets the needs of the moment. They can all become part of the leader's style repertoire.

- Visionary
- Coaching
- Affiliative
- Democratic
- Pacesetting
- Commanding

FIGURE 31 — PRIMAL LEADERSHIP STYLES

The core values of the organization will ultimately dictate the expectations around how its leaders lead, and the accountabilities assigned to leadership roles will define what is expected of them. Even when leaders adapt their styles to the situation, as discussed earlier, the culture of the organization will set the boundaries within which its leaders are expected to adapt to the situation. Great leaders have the ability to move their natural leadership style up and down the spectrum, from democratic to autocratic, based on the situation (Figure 32). The situation is a function of the type and urgency of the decision to be made, and the maturity, confidence, or competency level of team members. While great leaders will adjust to the situation, their natural or reflex leadership style needs to be within the known and generally accepted modern range, which I would argue is Level-5 leadership.

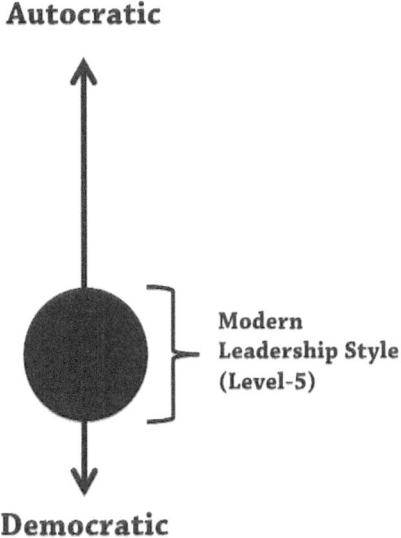

FIGURE 32 — SITUATIONAL LEADERSHIP SPECTRUM

The 1994 book *Improving Organizational Effectiveness Through Transformational Leadership*[19] by Bernard M. Bass gave birth to what is now known as the Transformational Leadership theory. It was set in contrast to so-called Transactional Leadership, which would probably better fit the legacy definition of a manager. The transformational leader takes on a far more inspirational and developmental role with their team members (Figure 33). The individualized consideration and the idealized influence relationship aspects of the transformational leader was further developed and became known as personal leadership by leadership gurus.

Intellectual Stimulation – Transformational leaders not only challenge the status quo; they also encourage creativity among followers. The leader encourages followers to explore new ways of doing things and new opportunities to learn.

Individualized Consideration – Transformational leadership also involves offering support and encouragement to individual followers. In order to foster supportive relationships, transformational leaders keep lines of communication open so that followers feel free to share ideas and so that leaders can offer direct recognition of each follower's unique contributions.

Inspirational Motivation – Transformational leaders have a clear vision that they are able to articulate to followers. These leaders are also able to help followers experience the same passion and motivation to fulfil these goals.

Idealized Influence – The transformational leader serves as a role model for followers. Because followers trust and respect the leader, they emulate the leader and internalize his or her ideals.

FIGURE 33 — TRANSFORMATIONAL LEADERSHIP CHARACTERISTICS

In his latest book, *The Leadership Code: Five Rules to Lead By*[20], leadership and HR effectiveness guru Dave Ulrich echoed other authors in stating what he sees as the essentials of modern leadership (Figure 34). Again, the dual theme of inspiring and developing others surfaces but with a clear focus on execution. The execution component of leadership is really what we call management nowadays.

1. Leaders must invest in themselves to be personally proficient. Effective leaders manage their physical, emotional, intellectual, and spiritual selves well. They learn constantly. They are capable of quick, bold actions as well as great patience. They constantly deepen their insight about themselves. This is especially true in tough economic times when people look to their leaders for hope and confidence.
2. Good leaders know how to be strategists and are able to answer the question "Where are we going?" They test their big ideas pragmatically, and they work with others to find the path from the present to the desired future.
3. Effective leaders are executors. They ask: "How will we ensure that we reach our goal?" They understand how to make change happen, assign accountability, delegate appropriately, and make sure that teams work well together.
4. These leaders are talent managers and engage people to get things done now and in a manner that generates intense personal, professional, and organizational loyalty. They help people bring their best to the job at hand.
5. Finally, they are human capital developers who build the next generation. They make sure that the organization has the longer-term skills, knowledge, behaviors and attitudes for future strategic success.

FIGURE 34 — FIVE RULES TO LEAD BY

To quote another renowned author regarding the basic difference between leadership and management, Steven Covey, author of *The Seven Habits of Highly Effective People*[21], says that: "Management is efficiency in climbing the ladder of success; leadership determines whether the ladder is leaning against the right wall. Effective leadership is putting first things first. Effective management is discipline, carrying it out."

Management

If leadership is about inspiring a team and its members, then management competency has to be about all of the other aspects of a role mandate. Leadership itself, either transformational or visionary, without management can only result in chaos and failure. Management is about the plan and the execution necessary to make the vision unfold.

In their broadest sense, management competencies apply to each and every colleague in the organization, and not only to those who we traditionally would have referred to as managers. What we historically meant by managers—the role not the title—were those who were accountable for a team of people. In most roles, when we think about it, incumbents manage a wide array of aspects of every day organizational life (Figure 35).

- Finance/Budgets
- Human Resources
- Time
- Physical Assets (space/equipment)
- Priorities
- Issues/Crises
- Data/Information/Metrics
- Relationships (interpersonal) & Communication
- Business Processes
- Projects
- Contracts

FIGURE 35 — MANAGEMENT OF WHAT?

There is one crossover between leadership and management when it comes to people. That is the competency related to an incumbent's ability to apply enough of the right human resources to a task, project or process. I used the term human resources here rather than people on purpose, to help create a distinction between the two. Some may argue that human resources management is embedded into either the project or process management sphere, or should be called resourcing. It could also be described as the people component which does not deal with the personal relationship between a team leader and team member.

It is probably useful to refer back to the legacy definition of what management is all about. The four components of management (Figure 36) can nicely be exploded into the previous list; each of them is one of the fundamental accountabilities of management.

- Plan
- Organize
- Direct
- Control

FIGURE 36 — TRADITIONAL MANAGEMENT ACCOUNTABILITIES

Functional

The functional or job family competency areas are those which also tend to map over the standard functional areas or sub-functions of an organization's structure, as we described earlier (Figure 4).

These functional areas tend to be referred to as subject-matter expertise areas. For example, the positions found in the finance sub-function tend to require deep proficiency in those functional competencies since it is there that functional processes are designed and optimized. However, most roles require a certain proficiency level in key functional areas, such as finance in this example, since financial processes are used by most colleagues. The budget process is a good example. Those competencies are normally tagged as managerial ones, common to all management roles.

Generally, the business enabling functions—Finance, HR, Business Technology, Legal—are those which find their functional processes embedded in most positions. As a rule of thumb, most of the steps in the organization's business-enabling processes require most colleagues in the organization to be proficient in that technical or functional competency area. This also explains why the accountability for ensuring that learning and development—or competency development—in the competencies related to a business enabling function is provided to all colleagues by the members of the relevant business-enabling function or team. The sales organization, for example, develops processes which are horizontal as well, but often do not touch each of the vertical functions and their respective roles.

Technical

The technical or professional competencies tend to be those which are related to a specific job within a family, such as the job of accountant, which is part of the finance job family or function for example.

Industrial

The reflex of most organizations is to deem that each incumbent be competent in whatever industrial sector the organization competes or operates *(I happen to disagree with this)*. We all have a tendency, particularly if our respective careers have been spent in one industry in particular, to believe—and indeed insist—that having spent many years in the industry is paramount to being successful in any role.

It would be difficult to argue that experience and competency in the industry is not a good thing to have. However, to insist on industry experience also means that the external recruitment of candidates becomes narrowed to one industry in particular. We have all seen the incestuous movement of individuals between competitors in some industries. The phenomenon precludes cross-pollination of talent between industry sectors, and leads to a weakening of the industry's gene pool. Furthermore, it may not be productive to hire an industry apostle when a critical shift in market or product strategy is in the making. Incidentally, choosing an external candidate from the same industry, as opposed to promoting from within has similar risks and benefits.

By definition, most serial entrepreneurs are never from the industry and somehow manage to be successful at creating businesses—or conglomerates—which are often in different industries. One very famous example would be the CEO and co-founder of Apple, the late Steve Jobs, who was not only successful at Apple with personal computers, but was also co-founder of Pixar animation (*Toy Story*), and lead the diversification of Apple with the launch of the iPod, iPhone, and iTunes music store (*In retrospect, Jobs was probably very competent in the 'digital consumer goods' industry*).

It is highly advisable, when defining a role and its competency requirements, to honestly ask ourselves why it is important for the incumbent to have industry competencies. We may be trading off a shorter industry learning curve for higher performance or innovation potential. In sales or revenue-generation roles, where the relationship with previous customers buying from the same industry is a definite asset, industry competency is definitely an asset. It is also a productive exercise to ask which other industry has similar particularities that could be transferable. For example, one may insist that all incumbents come from the beverage industry, rather than the food, or consumer product one, which have very similar characteristics.

Physical

Most of the roles we consider to be white collar do not really require any specific ability to carry out tasks of a physical nature, apart perhaps from international travel. Certain roles necessitate particular physical attributes such as the ability to lift a certain weight for a certain number of repetitions, to walk for a certain distance, have vision and auditory capabilities, or—in the case of pilots or astronauts—withstand severe gravitational forces. Those factors are known to be bona fide occupational requirements. While some of the physical competencies can be developed to higher levels of proficiency through training, others such as vision for example are innate to an individual at a point in time.

Linguistic

It is pretty well understood, in organizations, that the ability to effectively communicate amongst colleagues is paramount. The competency requirements will vary based on the role and its accountabilities. In some geographies or organizations—and particularly global ones—individuals are even expected to be able to communicate in more than one language. The ability to communicate in a particular language is defined in four components (Figure 37).

- Understand
- Speak
- Read
- Write

FIGURE 37 — LANGUAGE COMPETENCIES

The proficiency in each of the language competencies can also be defined, using the US Government Interagency Language Roundtable (ILR) five-level proficiency scale (Figure 38).

1. Elementary
2. Limited Working
3. Professional Working
4. Full Professional
5. Native/Bilingual

FIGURE 38 — LANGUAGE PROFICIENCY LEVELS

Technological

Now more than ever, an incumbent's ability to effectively use and leverage business technology is critical to role performance. The importance of technological competency is related to the need to quickly communicate and exchange information and to optimize and automate business processes and transactions for competitiveness reasons. Ideally, the incumbent would have direct competency in whichever systems are used by the organization. Nevertheless, many systems and software applications are very similar, and proficiency in one is more than likely very transferable to another. The various spreadsheet, word-processing and ERP software products are for the most part fairly similar.

ACADEMIC & PROFESSIONAL CREDENTIALS

I am often amazed that, in this day and age, some organizations still define academic qualifications or schooling as a requirement to perform a role, or use them as a proxy for competence. *(That being said, I happen to be a great believer though that education is kind of necessary in a 'knowledge economy').* We have all worked with people who were top-notch performers but did not have formal schooling. In most cases, they could have pursued their education, but personal or financial circumstances did not allow them to do so (*How about Henry Ford, Michael Dell and Steven Spielberg*). In too many cases, academic credentials only serve as a means of eliminating potential candidates for the position, which is often a reflection of the organization's deficient talent-acquisition capability.

I once worked for a narcissistic CEO who actually insisted that anyone we hired for senior-level positions have an MBA from one of the Ivy League schools. He had one and thought he was a genius, so he wanted to believe that everyone else who had one was also. Malcolm Gladwell, the author of *Outliers*[22] provided evidence that there is actually no correlation between success and Ivy League degrees, but rather the correlation is between graduating from a university or not. University students primarily acquire knowledge, and develop basic functional or technical competencies (*Including beer drinking*).

It is true that, in this rapidly changing environment, where the ability to learn is critical, some organizations also consider academic credentials as a reliable indicator of an individual's ability to learn, or their potential. And while it can be so, it is important to recognize that intellect alone won't necessarily get you ahead. It is clear that for entry-level roles, academic qualifications may be more relevant, for the individual would have gotten a functional head start, without the benefit of demonstrated performance in the role.

The professional designation is not only a confirmation of academic credentials, but most of the associations will require the completion of a practicum, stringent testing, and continuous professional development during the course of a career to ensure technical or functional competency. Most of the roles requiring a professional designation are highly technical ones, where it would be difficult for an organization to validate that the individual indeed has the required technical competencies. That is why the verification is left to the relevant professional associations. The certification or approval of certain technical tasks, such as financial statements or engineering plans for example—if those are accountabilities contained in the role profile—necessitates that the individual hold a designation.

PERSONALITY

Personality: The totality of an individual's behavioural and emotional characteristics. A set of distinctive traits and characteristics. The set of emotional qualities, ways of behaving that makes a person different from other people

The need to clearly determine which type of personality or motivational profile is required for any particular role is hinged on the concept that some personalities are better suited for certain roles than others. The way to achieve optimal performance or effectiveness—using a performance equation—is to assign incumbents to roles which suit them well in all aspects of the role, including personality. The only way to be clear when determining which personality is best suited for a role is to use a methodology or framework which enables the organization to do that.

The personality of an individual defines the individual's emotional reflexes—the type of role they enjoy performing. Who they are as a person is determined by a combination of their personality and personal values. Think of Nelson Mandela and Saddam Hussein, who could have had similar personalities, but with dichotomously opposed sets of personal values, resulting in very different behaviours.

Behaviour = (Stimulus) X (Personality + Values)

Several models and concepts exist to define and nickname personality types. Psychologists and researchers have developed ways to do so, which are commercially available to organizations. By far, one of the most popular of those psychometric instruments is the Myers-Briggs Type Indicator (MBTI) questionnaire, which many other tools are based on as well (*I am not trying to sell it to you*). The particular tool used is almost irrelevant, as long as the organization uses a simple and formal framework. The MBTI uses four pairs of preferences or dichotomies—Either/Or—to tag someone's personality type, which is then expressed as a series of 4 letters (Figure 39).

Preference	Letter	Vs.	Letter	Preference
Extroversion	(E)		(I)	Introversion
Sensing	(S)		(N)	Intuition
Thinking	(T)		(F)	Feeling
Judging	(J)		(P)	Perception

FIGURE 39 — MBTI DICHOTOMIES

Some other questionnaires will tag personality types using descriptors, colours, graphical representation, or even animals (*Shark should be one of them*) to make it easier to refer to one personality type or another. The Predictive

Index™ questionnaire, for example, provides an easy way to determine the type of personality required, by using a high/low scale for each of four factors (Figure 40). Each of the four factors is plotted on a normal distribution curve to show the level of the factor relative to a sample population. The behaviours associated with the personality type are arrived at by developing a composite view of all factors put together.

A. **Dominance:** The degree to which an individual seeks to control his or her environment
B. **Extraversion:** The degree to which an individual seeks social interaction with other people
C. **Patience:** The degree to which an individual seeks consistency and stability in his or her environment
D. **Formality:** The degree to which an individual seeks to conform to formal rules and structure

FIGURE 40 — PREDICTIVE INDEX® FACTORS

Most of these psychometric tools come with both a role or job-evaluation questionnaire, designed to identify what personality is best suited for the role and an incumbent/candidate questionnaire to determine the person's actual motivational profile. The user can then simply overlay the individual's personality profile on the role profile and determine the match.

There is another category of psychometric instruments, which are considered to be the 'pro-series' tools, for they are more powerful and predictive. These tools can only be administered by certified psychologists who typically work for assessment consulting firms. The Big Five factors of personality (Figure 41) have become common jargon in the psychometric world and a standard in personality assessment.

There are also 'derailers' which describe personality traits which can be counterproductive to performance. Those derailers range from being arrogant, to micro managing, impulsive, or volatile.

Factor	Trait	Vs.	Trait	Definition
Openness	Inventive Curious		Consistent Cautious	Appreciation for art, emotion, adventure, unusual ideas, curiosity, and variety of experience
Conscientiousness	Efficient Organized		Easy-going Careless	A tendency to show self-discipline, act dutifully, and aim for achievement; planned rather than spontaneous behavior
Extraversion	Outgoing Energetic		Solitary Reserved	Energy, positive emotions, surgency, and the tendency to seek stimulation in the company of others
Agreeableness	Friendly Compassionate		Cold Unkind	A tendency to be compassionate and cooperative rather than suspicious and antagonistic towards others
Neuroticism	Sensitive Nervous		Secure Confident	A tendency to experience unpleasant emotions easily, such as anger, anxiety, depression, or vulnerability

FIGURE 41 — BIG FIVE PERSONALITY TRAITS OR OCEAN

In organizations, we often refer to these individual traits or combinations of them when describing a personality type, candidate, or colleague. We will describe an individual as 'type A' or a 'people' person or a multitasker or as detail-oriented. The latter can sometimes be problematic. Some roles demand high precision and thoroughness, while others don't. These detail-oriented characters most often struggle as leaders and delegators, for they are petrified of the risk of error inherent to delegation. The truth is that personalities and types are actual trade-offs, and nobody can have all of those traits; they are often either/or dichotomies or at one end or the other of the normal spectrum.

We probably spend way too much time arguing about how and when personalities are formed. The truth is that, by the time the individual enters the workforce, their personality is formed and stays. Some will argue that it is worth it to attempt to change colleagues with personality issues or dysfunctionalities. I am not convinced of this. Development and awareness will somewhat soften up the edges of a disorder, but fundamental change only occurs over a long period of time and through significant emotional events. Organizations should not get in the business of therapy and behavioural modification (*Although some of the characters I worked with would have made for great research subjects*).

COGNITIVE INTELLIGENCE

Intelligence:	The ability to learn or understand or to deal with a new or trying situation. The skilled use of reason. The act of understanding
Reason:	The power of comprehending, inferring, or thinking especially in orderly rational ways

The topic of intellectual capability or IQ is a sensitive one in business and for good reason. It would be somewhat controversial (*And that is an understatement*) to state the IQ requirement for each role in the organization. Of course we know that some roles require a higher intellect (*Or cognitive intelligence or ability if you are looking for a softer term*) than others. What really matters is the incumbent's ability to perform the role and their ability to learn and acquire new competencies, which is in turn driven by their intellectual capability. It is far more useful to speak in terms of relevant competencies, such as problem-solving ability, than it is to focus on IQ (Figure 42). Some organizations still administer cognitive intelligence tests to candidates and potential incumbents in order to predict their ability to acquire competencies, or potential.

Problem Solving:
Identifies and analyzes problems; weighs relevance and accuracy of information; generates and evaluates alternative solutions; makes recommendations

FIGURE 42 — PROBLEM SOLVING
COMPETENCY DESCRIPTOR

We also make the assumption that someone with a certain level of academic credentials has sufficient intellectual capability to perform a role and learn. There is definitely a correlation, but it is not a perfect one; it would suggest, for instance, that all individuals without academic credentials have limited intellectual capability. Intellect is an individual's CPU and probably one of the best four predictors of leadership potential, along with personality, values and emotional intelligence. It is surprising just how many performance issues are related to an individual's inability to quickly learn and acquire new competencies.

EMOTIONAL INTELLIGENCE

The notion of emotional intelligence or EQ came about in the mid-1980s, particularly when discussing issues related to team-leadership roles, where interpersonal relationships are mission critical. If IQ measures the ability to understand things, then EQ is about the ability to understand, decode, and predict people with their feelings and emotions. Once again, SMEs will argue the models and the theories of Emotional Intelligence, but what is really impactful to an organization its awareness of the concept and the use of a workable model.

For the purpose of distinguishing one from the other, I will use cognitive intelligence and emotional intelligence as the two components of intelligence. Cognitive intelligence can be replicated in robots—commonly referred to as artificial intelligence—but the emotional component cannot be transposed (*Think of Data, the Star Trek android*). In the measurement of EQ, it is important to remember that no individual scores zero. Some people merely have higher EQ than others. As in the case of IQ, psychometric tests can be used to measure the level at which a person operates. There is as much controversy and sensitivity around measuring EQ as there is around IQ.

It logically follows that a role which requires the leadership of other colleagues, frequent client interactions, or negotiations with individuals or groups, may require a higher level of Emotional Intelligence. As it is with IQ, it is again easier—and far less controversial—for organizations to define EQ requirements by way of relevant competencies rather than a pure quotient measurement. Consulting firms and providers, such as HayGroup® have developed clusters of competencies which make up Emotional Intelligence (Figure 43).

Cluster	Competencies	
Self-Awareness	Emotional Self-Awareness	Accurate Self-Assessment
	Self-Confidence	
Self-Management	Self-Control	Trustworthiness
	Conscientiousness	Adaptability
	Achievement Orientation	Initiative
Social Awareness	Empathy	Organizational Awareness
	Service Orientation	
Social Skills	Developing Others	Leadership
	Influence	Communication
	Change Catalyst	Conflict Management
	Building Blocks	Teamwork and Collaboration

FIGURE 43 — HAYGROUP® EMOTIONAL COMPETENCY INVENTORY

VALUES & BELIEFS

The core values of the organization, as we discussed earlier, are not only a common requirement for all positions, but are also critical to teamwork. They simply need to be stated as a template on all role profiles, and also find their way on each profile as core competencies.

HIERARCHY LEVEL & ROLE PROFILE

In a standard organization structure—most likely depicted as a pyramid with the CEO at the top—positions get impacted in a similar way when gaining organizational altitude.

This is what occurs:

1. The weight of accountability increases
2. The total compensation and position grade increase
3. Roles evolve from managing self to leading:
    - Team members
    - Teams and team leaders
    - Single Function
    - Multiple/cross functions
    - Single Business Unit
    - General Managers
    - The entire organization
4. The breadth increases and depth reduces
5. Accountabilities migrate from operational to tactical to strategic
6. Scope of mandates go from local to global
7. The issues radar goes from close range to over-the-horizon
8. Impact of decisions goes from hours to decades
9. Life goes from brutal reality of operations to Disneyland fairy-tale of corporate office (*Ivory tower altitude-induced hypoxia tends to make senior leaders delusional and lose track of reality. That's why they should not stay there too long and should try to get some oxygen back on earth where they can observe real colleagues and customers in their natural habitat*)

EXPECTATIONS FOR THE ROLE

The expectations for any given role are broadly stated in the role mandate and then more specifically in the list of key accountabilities assigned to the role. Those cover the base or foundation or day-to-day business. At any given point in time, and generally every year, new expectations are set for the entire organization as it refreshes its business strategy and sets new goals. The flow down or cascading of that process permeates every role with a new set of expectations for the year.

PERFORMANCE OBJECTIVES

Those new yearly expectations are translated into performance objectives assigned to the role. Those goals are most likely broken down in two distinct categories: strategic goals, which clearly can be linked to the organization's overall business strategy; and breakthrough goals, which pertain to making important improvement to the base business by addressing a significant process or business issue. Breakthrough goals tend to be related to one of the organization's core values. Some organizations dictate that any goal or initiative outside of strategic goals needs to clearly add value for the customers; otherwise it is not deemed to be needed.

CRITICAL SUCCESS FACTORS

The factors which are likely to make the fulfillment of the role accountabilities and achievement of the performance objectives possible or those factors which could prevent the incumbent from being successful are considered to be critical success factors. The factors which will enable a new incumbent to onboard effectively both with their horizontal and vertical team as well as other stakeholders, can also be deemed critical.

It is useful to develop those as they provide for a more focused view on which elements of the position profile are most important. These elements can be those selection criteria with the heaviest weight when considering candidates for the role. Of course, the tendency is to deem any and every factor to be critical, which defeats the purpose of the distinction.

WHAT THE ROLE IS WORTH

GRADE

The grade of a position is really what dictates the total compensation attached to it. Grade is determined to ensure both internal equity amongst roles and employment-market competitiveness. The incumbent, or potential candidates, want to know how they will get paid and understand the relationship between their individual and team's performance and the rewards or incentive they will receive.

TITLE

In any organization, we have to keep track of positions, either by calling the position by its name or, in some cases, a numerical or inventory descriptor. We also need the title to advertise it, insert it on organizational charts, or to print it on business cards. It makes sense, as we need to define or brand the role in some way. If the mandate of the position is the position profile's lead paragraph, the title is its short version or headline, combined with some kind of hierarchy denominator.

It is often very difficult for organizations to resist the temptation to come up with position titles which have three or four components to them. Often that is because they want to list all of the sub-functions of the team, rather than use the team's composite function nomenclature. Fortunately, most are constrained by the size of a standard business card. The job title should succinctly answer the following question: 'So, what do you do for the organization?' Leave it to the position mandate and profile to better or fully describe the position and provide the elevator pitch for the role. Customers and colleagues should more or less be able to intuit the position by simply looking at the business card. They can wait for lunch (*Or elevator ride on the way there*) for the full conversation around the actual role.

We all have this need to understand who fits where in the organizational hierarchy, so we came up with levels starting with Chief: Chief Executive Officer (CEO), Chief Financial Officer (CFO), Chief Operations Officer (COO), etc. Next comes President, and the Vice Presidents, etc. (Figure 44). (*Bankers have mastered the art of adding more levels to the Vice President title. It makes their customers feel more important that way*). We can qualify each of the levels with either executive, senior, assistant, regional, group and so on. These titles typically will apply to some kind of a business unit, region, or customer segment—which explains why there can be many Presidents or Directors of Finance, each being accountable for a different unit. Very large organizations, global organizations for instance, had no option but to come up with a lot of levels, due to their sheer size.

One of the best hierarchy or level title systems is the one used by the military or police. These organizations employ ranks. The beauty of the military is that, even before business cards are handed out, the uniform is already a pretty good descriptor for the role level, for the ranks are right there on the shoulders or arms (*Military dictators add a few gold stripes and things to look even more important*). The titles are typically aligned to pay or total compensation grades, for they tend to reflect the weight of accountability attached to each role.

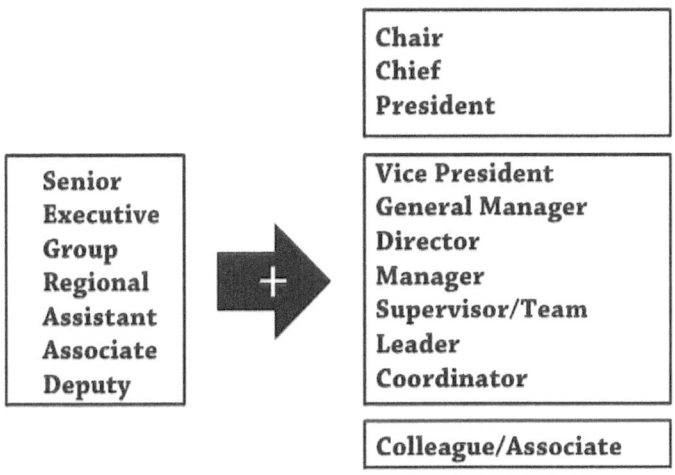

FIGURE 44 — POSITION TITLES

There is rarely a need for organizations to invent a title; the industry or employment market invariably does a better job at developing them. Not only does this make it easier for industry colleagues to quickly correlate each other's accountability set, but it is also important to potential incumbents or candidates who need to show career progression on their resume. In global organizations, it is often a challenge to align titles, for different geographies and culture use different norms. A good example of this is the use of Managing Director in several European countries as a proxy for CEO. These organizations tend to use internal titles such as Country Manager while the business card title may read CEO, President or Managing Director.

THE RIGHT WORKSHOP

In order for the incumbent to adequately fulfil the mandate of the position, its accountabilities, and performance objectives, they need to have the right tools and resources and be capable of operating in the associated work environment.

WORK TOOLS

The tools and resources assigned to a position or role (Figure 45) can be put into two separate categories: those which are required to fulfil the mandate of the position and its accountabilities and those which are necessary to complete the projects or tasks linked to yearly performance objectives. They are often referred to as base and breakthrough resources respectively.

- People (regular, FTE's, consultants)
- Budget (base, discretionary, capital)
- Physical Space/Facilities
- Tools/Technology
- Time
- Information/Data

FIGURE 45 — RESOURCES ALLOCATED

PHYSICAL WORK ENVIRONMENT

We often forget that the quality and suitability of the physical environment in which a role is to be performed may have a significant impact on the level of performance—not to mention on occupational health and safety. The impact of environmental factors may vary depending on the incumbent (Figure 46).

- Ambient Temperature
- Physical Security/Safety
- Ergonomics
- Wearing of Protective Gear
- Ambient Noise
- Spatial Lay-out
- Travel Requirement
- Air Quality

FIGURE 46 — ENVIRONMENTAL FACTORS

THE TALENT SYSTEM

We discussed earlier the need for the organization to develop a sound business strategy and determine the culture and values it needs to be successful at executing the strategy. The business strategy would have a People or Talent Strategy annex inevitably outlining the important and long-range people initiatives as well as issues which would need to be developed and launched or addressed in support of the achievement of the business strategy (*I am sure some still don't, but I would be curious to know how well they are doing*). The strategic initiatives would most likely be aligned under each of HR's functional Key Accountability Areas (KAAs).

The people policies or guidelines are derived from the stated organizational values and outline how we will deal with issues related to people within the organization (*The term Guidelines is more modern, and carries the notion of flexibility and simplicity*). They are statements of intent which need to be clear to all. Effectively, what they say is: this is the way we do business. They are to the organization's culture what laws are to societal values. The HR team does not own these policies, but they manage them, and they reflect how colleagues and team leaders will deal with each other regarding people matters. The policies are recommended by the top HR leader and decided upon by the Chief Executive after debate around the top leadership team's table.

In the people business, there are a few key business processes which support the effective management of the colleague population's career lifecycle (Figure 47) during their career tenure within the organization. The intent here is not to map out detailed processes (*I will leave that to the text book people*), but rather to discuss the key features, integration points and pitfalls to avoid.

- Contemplating
- Joining
- On-boarding
- Performing
- Learning/Developing
- Progressing/Advancing
- Off-boarding
- Reminiscing

FIGURE 47 — CAREER LIFECYCLE STAGES

ROLE PROFILING—CLEARLY DEFINING WHAT IS NEEDED

The profiling of new roles, or the significant modification of an existing one, is a process in and of itself, which culminates in the publication of a role profile. Ideally, these profiles are accessible to all colleagues, for which either an internal or external candidate will become the incumbent. The process is, in fact, one of the cornerstones of the organization, for it defines each of the building blocks making up its teams, which in turn make up the organization.

The process begins with the understanding of the rationale and context for the role—why the business and teams need to create this role. It is inevitably anchored in either an initiative contained in the business plan, the creation of a new process or its significant modification, insufficient capacity, or it is intended to address an issue or opportunity which has somehow surfaced. Personally, I could never understand why, in such a dynamic environment, organizations insist on creating new positions only at budget time. Budgets are best-guess guides only. We don't wait until next year to create incremental revenues, do we? So why do we have to wait until next year to incur unbudgeted new expenses if they are necessary?

The decision to create a new role is a significant one, not only from a total direct cost, overhead, or future severance liability, but also for the impact the new role will have on the organization. The incumbent will understandably want to launch initiatives and secure an incremental budget (*Finance types will love me on this one*). The worst-case scenario is the creation of a new role followed by the hiring or assignment of an incumbent, only then to discover it was not a good idea, for it would not only be disruptive for the organization, but also pejorative on the new incumbent's career plan, particularly if the person's employment is terminated as a result, or the person had resigned from a previous organization to take on this new role.

In order to clearly understand how the new position will dovetail into the existing organization, it is important to review the surrounding positions—roles within the horizontal and vertical teams, as well as the position's team leader's role. In developing the new position's accountability cluster, it is possible that some accountabilities or performance objectives may have to be combed out of certain roles. The creation of a new role is also an opportunity to review performance gaps in the surrounding roles and assign the related accountabilities to the new role.

Once a draft profile is developed, a mini change-management plan, using a formal framework, needs to be developed. This includes assessing the impact of the new role on other incumbents and consultation with stakeholders. The final role profile is then reviewed and approved by those who have the authority to approve, according to the role profiling and creation process. Typically this includes the team leader, their team leader, as well as someone from Finance and HR.

TALENT ACQUISITION—GETTING THE RIGHT PEOPLE FOR THE ROLE... QUICKLY

The process of bringing in the right people or talent into the organization has become a bigger challenge in recent years, starting with the infamous *War for Talent*[23] report published by the management consulting firm McKinsey & Company in 1997. The sad reality is that organizations probably would have not gotten on board with it had the report been prepared by an HR consulting firm. In today's knowledge-based economy, with the Baby Boomers retiring, organizations are finally figuring out that people are indeed their most valuable asset. For this reason, it is felt that time and money are well spent ensuring that the right people for the role are brought on board (*An employment or career relationship is like a marriage; they are hard enough to make work, so you'd better start with the right one*).

Gen-Xers and Millennials, with an average job tenure of 3–5 years and 2–4 years respectively—as opposed to 6–12 years for the Baby Boomers—compound this challenge, for they are far more mobile, consider themselves free agents, and are not so willing to stay the course when faced with better options. The challenge of talent acquisition is even more daunting in high-growth industries (Technology), high-turnover industries (Retail) and unattractive organizations or industries (Tobacco).

The employment and job market is very similar to any other product market, where the buyer of talent is the organization, and the buyer of career is the candidate. The currency used by the organization is rewards, learning, and career progression, while the candidates pay with their performance and contribution to the organization's success. The deal or value proposition is about the relationship between the value that colleagues are expected to create for the organization and the value they can expect in return. The concept of mass career customization—or its predecessor, flexible total compensation—was developed to effectively enable individuals to customize their careers and subsequent rewards to suit their personal needs, and consequently enhance its value to the individual. The phenomenon is similar to a consumer buying a car and paying for an accessory they have no use for. The option would therefore be considered to be of minimal or no value. The perceived value of the car goes up if all of the options paid for are those wanted by the buyer.

The ability of an organization to attract the right people is not only a function of the effectiveness of its recruiting machine and the availability of candidates, but also its reputation and visibility in the employment market. We now use the term 'employment brand' to describe it. The application of brand management marketing techniques to human resource management was tested by Simon Barrow, chairman of People in Business, and Tim Ambler, Senior Fellow of London Business School, in the Journal of Brand Management in December of 1996[24]. Several other authors subsequently studied and discussed the need to align the external or product brand to the employment one in order to effectively deliver the promise to customers. For instance, you can't have a product or brand experience which claims to be fun, and have customer-facing colleagues with no sense of humour, who are not having fun working for the organization, or not using its product.

In this era of personal technology and social networking, it is incredibly easy for technically savvy candidates to find out about the work environment of a potential employer. There are several blogs on the net where current and past colleagues can go to discuss and rate their career experience with an organization (*I am not sure why industry should expect compelling employment branding initiatives to magically emanate from HR teams with limited employment or career-marketing and branding competencies!*).

Many organizations choose to participate in so called 'Best Companies to Work For' surveys, and use the certification symbol on their career marketing material. The marketing value is good, but I have worked for—as the head of HR no less—an organization which had made it onto such a list, and most of us could not figure out how we got there! There is a fundamental principle in customer satisfaction which says that it is always best to manage the customer's expectations by not over selling and subsequently disappointing the customer with the actual experience. The same concept is true in career selling or recruiting. Branding your organization as the best place to work in the industry, when it's not really warranted, can disappoint new hires and create on-boarding, engagement and retention issues.

The first logical step in the acquisition process is to determine if there are internal candidates who may be available, which is why, in addition to looking at the talent plan, every opportunity should be communicated internally. With career opportunities and development being two of the key drivers of colleague engagement, it is wise and advisable to promote as many colleagues as possible, rather than parachute an external candidate in. Whenever an external hire must be brought in, the organization's reflex should be to ask itself why no internal candidate was available and check its talent planning process or program. That being said, it is healthy to regularly inject fresh DNA in the organization's gene pool, so to speak, by having one out of four or five individuals coming from outside the organization.

The process of interviewing internal candidates who have indicated their interest for a position is a healthy one, for it assumes that the candidate who best fits the position profile should be offered the opportunity. The practice of interviewing internal and external candidates simultaneously is a dangerous one and naively supports the notion that the organization means to hire the best talent available either within the organization or on the employment market. We forget that the purpose is to select a person who fits the profile and ideally has the best potential to advance and progress; that decision is easily made internally. It is a fallacy to believe that any external sourcing process leads to an absolute identification of best talent. The reality is that it identifies nothing more than the best talent currently available, aware, and interested in the position. I don't believe that our job is to hire the best people. What we strive to do is hire the right people for the right role, or as Jim Collins said *"getting the right people on the bus"*[15]. External candidates should only be considered once the organization has determined that either no internal candidate is suitable, or that new DNA is required in the gene pool.

It is always tempting for organizations to first attempt to recruit externally, so as to avoid the potential disruption of the resulting domino effect, wherein each internal promotion requires a follow-up posting to fill the subsequently vacated position. The perceived ease of such a decision is illusory, for the potential disruption pales in comparison to the risks of new-hire integration and the cost of employee disengagement associated with the perceived lack of consideration for internal candidates.

There is also another phenomenon at work, one which can be summed this way: The candidate we know always looks worse than the one we don't. It is important to remember that this is only because we know the weaknesses of internal candidates, but not the weaknesses of the external ones. A study conducted by business consultants Booz Allen in 2008 revealed that more than 20 percent of all CEOs are brought in from outside the company, even though outsiders in North America and Europe, on average, significantly underperform compared to those individuals promoted to the role of CEO from inside.

There is also the risk of internal candidates remaining frozen in time, for we remember them when they first joined the organization and forget that they have matured and developed since. Not entirely unlike your adult children, who at age 40 still feel to you as they did when they were teenagers.

The development of a staffing strategy is key to the process of acquiring the right talent quickly. The balanced need for both speed and quality in recruiting a candidate is justified by the fact that, while the position is vacant, the position accountabilities and performance objectives attached to it are either not being fulfilled, or are being added to the plate of another colleague, who may or may not have the time and competencies to get them done. The strategy will outline how the organization's recruiters will reach the right potential candidates for the role. It will demonstrate an understanding of where those candidates work and live, and where they seek career opportunity information. The recruiters are those individuals who are the image of the organization to the employment market—the career opportunities salespeople. The ambassadors and competent cultural role models, who not only come up with the recruiting plans, but also close talent deals. They are just as important as your product, customer service, or sales force (*In fact, they recruit them*). The recruiters, either internal or external, don't decide who gets hired, but rather screen out or censor the list of potential candidates, which is why they should have the utmost integrity, objectivity, and personal bias awareness.

The art of reaching candidates, who are not currently seeking a different career opportunity, and selling them on the idea of considering one, is often left to recruitment or executive search consultants. Formerly known as headhunters, these are the individuals to whom the recruitment process is often outsourced. Recruitment consultants are really brokers who represent their client in selling their career opportunities to potential candidates in return for a fee. There are a few aspects of that industry which should be of concern to organizations (*And I am being facetious here*).

Why would you trust the outsourcing of one of the most critical elements of the organization's success to an external firm? They are traditionally staffed by former sales people with minimal recruitment or selection competencies, let alone professional HR designations. They typically charge exorbitant fees—20 to 30 percent of the role's annual target cash compensation.

Most alarmingly, according to Michael Watkins the author of *The First 90 Days*[25], they will recommend the hiring of candidates who, 58 percent of the time will fail in their new position within 18 months! Perhaps this failure rate is related to the fact that candidates are being oversold on a career opportunity they were not seeking to begin with. My opinion was further reinforced by reading the research on the executive recruitment industry conducted by Monika Hamori, a Professor of Human Resource Management at the IE Business School in Madrid.

With that being said, it would not be fair to paint all recruitment consultants with the same brush. There are pure play recruitment consultants out there, with whom I have done business, who are highly competent, ethical, and process driven. They tend to be independent and specialized boutique firms, or very unique individuals who work for the larger global firms.

With the powerful research and communication capabilities of the internet and social networking sites, why delegate the task of finding career customers to a third party and subjugate one's employment brand? Candidates can easily locate career opportunities globally using powerful job-search engines, and colleagues can leverage their vast social network by referring personal contacts as potential new hires (*And please, whatever you do, refrain from asking candidates to fill out painful electronic career forms. Just get them to send their resume, and you do the rest!*).

According to a 2011 survey conducted by recruitment strategists CareerXroads, 27.5 percent of all new hires are identified through referrals, making it the top source of talent. For this reason, Employee Referral Programs are probably the best way to identify new talent. The candidates get a true picture of the environment, which prevents unrealistic expectations, and the colleagues assess their cultural fit. Not only that, they will also support their on-boarding once hired.

The selection and screening of potential candidates and their credentials can now be accomplished using a combination of online questionnaires, interviews, and psychometric assessment tools tailored to the position profile. I am a big fan of asking online applicants to answer questions related to the role profile, rather than simply relying on what is typically on the resume. The technology allows the organization to keep in touch with its career customers, and any contact with a potential customer is an opportunity to promote the brand, so respond to every applicant, and delete from your posting the phrase: 'Only those selected for an interview will be contacted.'

Despite the advancements in online information, the reviewing of resumes remains the essential component in the screening process. It is the candidate's career-marketing brochure. The experience (*Which is nothing but 'assumed' competency*) and achievements are almost always straightforward. What the recruiters try to do is figure out personality, values, and potential fit—which can sometimes be glimpsed by reviewing hobbies and interests as well as community involvement and affiliations. They try to interpret potential by looking at how fast the candidate has progressed, the breadth and depth of the assignments, and the quality of the organizations. A word of caution on job hoppers; the average tenure is coming down significantly, and what matters is why the person left the role, rather than having left or not.

Some organizations will send the final candidates for Chief-level or mission-critical roles to external assessment centres or consulting firms, which will run a series of psychological assessments and simulations. These centres are capable of extrapolating the scenario results into predictive assessments of competencies and proficiencies. The assessment of potential is necessary, but tricky. The need to assess a future colleague's potential is related to the talent planning process when the organization attempts to predict how far the individual can go. It is wise to acquire talent with great potential, for the growth of the organization and the demands and complexity of roles will certainly increase with time. Making sure the incumbent has the ability to learn and change quickly is like making sure your computer has a powerful enough CPU and sufficient RAM to accommodate heavier future applications.

The interviewing of candidates, after they have been pre-screened, is a significant investment of time for the organization. The purpose of the process is to validate the candidate's fit with the position profile and career interest. It also affords the benefit of being able to observe the candidate's body language and demeanour (*Not to determine what the person looks like*). The interview questions should be structured around the stated profile's competencies, using the modern technique of behavioural or competency-based interviewing. The technique consists of asking candidates for real-life examples of when they displayed the competency or behaviour.

The determination and verification of an individual's core values is probably the trickiest part of the screening process. How do you find out how honest or respectful an individual really is? I learned from one of the best executive selection people in the business that a significant emotional response to a question or statement is generally a great indicator of having poked at a person's core value.

During an interview, he would ask a person how honest they were on a scale from one to ten. Regardless of their answer he would either respond, 'Why so low?' or 'Why so high?' and then wait for an emotional reaction (*If someone answers '10', don't hire them. They are either lying or delusional*). He would then ask under what condition a person would choose to lie or cheat. His other favourite questions were: "How do you choose your friends?" and "What do you admire about them?" These he felt would provide for a good view of an individual's own values outlook, for friends typically share the same core values. In the end, it is easy for a candidate to state that they value or believe in any of the organization's core values. The real question is: Does the candidate have the courage of their convictions, and will they defend and respect them when under pressure?

High-performance organizations will insist that final candidates meet with members of both their vertical and horizontal teams—including the team's leader and their team leader. This supports the two signatures/levels on the check approach and provides an early talent management and planning perspective.

This approach provides team members with an opportunity to buy in or have a say in the hire, which is likely to entice them to support the success of the candidate's team integration and tenure with the organization. Let's not underestimate the usefulness of the process to the candidate, who also needs to determine if they want to join the team as well. While the decision to hire rests with the team leader and can only be vetoed by their team leader, other team members will provide their assessment and input. Their observations and concerns, as well as assessment results, will serve as some of the raw material for reference checking and will inform the candidate's on-boarding program and possibly their development plan as well.

I am a big fan of asking everyone who interviews a candidate to complete a common assessment relative to the critical components of the role profile. Contrary to what many hiring team leaders wishfully believe, it is virtually inevitable that none of the candidates will match the profile perfectly. This is why each of the critical components should be weighted relative to the others. The compiled results, which should not be considered mathematically valid, serve as a great tool during the process debrief session, leading to the decision on who to hire. It also helps in dealing with the cloning phenomenon, whereby the team leaders will naturally favour candidates who most closely resembles themselves.

Whether considering an external or internal candidate for a role, the key is to identify the match between the candidate and the requirements of the role. The better the fit, the better the performance in the role will be. The Role Fit© elements (Figure 48) are the individual aspects the incumbent brings to the role and which will drive performance.

The competencies gaps between the incumbent and the role profile are developmental opportunities which can be supported by a development plan. The other three fit elements can't really be truly developed as they define who the incumbent fundamentally is at the reflex level (*The incumbent can learn to behave in an artificial way, but will burn a significant amount of energy in a futile attempt to do so sustainably*). The organization has to accept the fit gap and manage its performance and behavioural risk impacts.

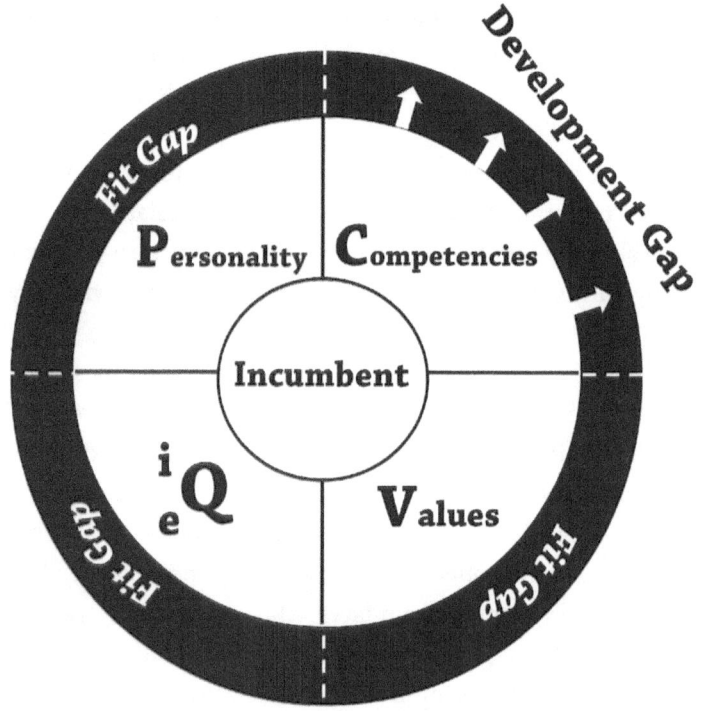

FIGURE 48 — ROLE FIT© MODEL

The final step in the process is to validate what the candidate's resume, interview, and assessment revealed by

conducting a reference check. There are a few fallacies in the process:
- The references provided by the candidates are biased. Would you provide references who are not likely to sing your praises to a potential employer? Best to find your own references.
- Many former employers are reluctant to be candid because of privacy legislation.
- The recruitment consultants naturally want to close the deal, so they tend to distort the process. It's always better to ask an independent third party.
- The reference checks are rarely based on what was uncovered or revealed during the selection process, or relative to the role profile, since the screening process is most often flawed and the role profile rarely exists.
- The more senior the role, the more reluctant organizations are to verify references, and so they rely on anecdotes and legends, which helps explain why so many low-quality executives continue to get selected.

ON-BOARDING—HITTING THE GROUND RUNNING... WITHOUT TRIPPING

There is a lot of data and evidence out there to suggest that the process of an individual taking on a new role is fraught with risks and inefficiencies. While it is true for internal candidates taking on a new role, it is even more so for external hires who not only have to integrate to a new role but also with a vertical and horizontal team and a new organization altogether. Assuming that a new incumbent is by definition never a perfect match, there will be gaps at many levels.

The fundamental purpose of on-boarding is to mitigate the risks of these gaps and ensure that the new hire learns and performs the role optimally as quickly as possible as well as to ensure that the candidate lands smoothly in the organization, without damaging relationships and perceptions. Michael Watkins, the author of *The first 90 Days*[25], offers a great framework (Figure 49) to design on-boarding programs. The key to being successful is to have identified the gaps between the new incumbent and the role profile during the selection and reference processes, design a formal on-boarding program, and assign clear accountabilities to the stakeholders for its execution.

I would propose here that for any new person to join a team—and the more senior the position the truer it is—is potentially a significant change. The parallels between a change management framework (Figure 49), in this case the one developed by John Kotter in *Leading Change*[26] and an on-boarding one are not surprising. This means that it would probably be wise to develop a change-management plan to accompany the assignment of a new colleague to a new role, particularly if that new role will substantially impact the organization, such as a new Chief-level individual or the leader of a strategic project.

Watkins (On-Boarding)	Kotter (Change)
• Promote yourself (out of your previous role) • Accelerate your learning • Match strategy to situation • Secure early wins • Negotiate success (with your new team leader) • Achieve alignment • Build your team • Create coalitions • Keep your balance (between professional and personal life) • Expedite everyone (with their own on-boarding)	• Establishing a sense of urgency • Forming a powerful guiding coalition • Creating a vision • Communicating the vision • Empowering others to act on the vision • Planning for and creating short-term wins • Consolidating improvements and producing more change • Institutionalizing new approaches

FIGURE 49 — ON-BOARDING AND CHANGE-MANAGEMENT FRAMEWORKS

PERFORMANCE DEVELOPMENT—HELPING PEOPLE DEVELOP AND PERFORM BETTER

The performance development program and process is at the heart of any high-performance team as it represents the systematic way by which each team leader will support colleagues in getting better at performing their role (*Kind of goes without saying, doesn't it?*). Developing performance is about continuously improving and getting better at fulfilling a role and ultimately getting ready to take on more accountabilities or moving on to the next role. In the past, the idea of performance assessment was exactly that. The boss would unilaterally assess the employee to first determine if they would keep the job, then get more money for doing it, or get promoted (*Still done that way in legacy or archaic organizations*).

No wonder team leaders struggled with, if not feared, the whole process in the past. They were asked to pass a highly subjective judgement on their own people, effectively playing judge and jury, without the benefit of other inputs. They were put in the position of judging individual performance relative to an unclear and ill-conceived role profile—if one even existed—with a cumbersome program designed by some technocrat who likely never had to use it, and all without adequate training.

Performance: Used to describe how effective or successful someone or something is. To do an action or activity that usually requires training or skill. How well someone or something functions, works

The modern organization understands that the intent of a performance program is for a team leader and a team member to candidly discuss and agree on a plan of action to rapidly increase the member's output. Through such discussions they can jointly determine if the execution of a plan is working, and then reward and recognize the member for having achieved it, all the while respecting the organization's core values.

Our human reflex is always to focus on fixing what is broken. I was only recently reacquainted with the appreciative enquiry concept by my hairstylist, who is big fan. Developed by David Cooperrider, appreciative enquiry focuses on enhancing or leveraging the things we do well rather than focusing on those we do not. The concept's mantra states that an organization is a miracle to be embraced rather than a problem to be solved. It supports notions of strategic and core competencies, and the so-called "sweet spot and hedgehog concepts"[13].

The performance of a colleague is measured against the accountabilities contained in their role profile, but also on the agreed-upon performance objectives for the year (*Humorously called the 'day job' and the 'evening shift' respectively*). The performance feedback is relative to what is expected of the person, based on their proficiency level. As an example, the performance of a brand new incumbent—who is being remunerated accordingly less—cannot be measured against a long-tenure incumbent. Some organizations insist on measuring incumbents using that yardstick, and proceed with assigning a 'needs improvement or development' performance rating to high performers who they just promoted in the role (*Not exactly an award-winning motivational idea*). The underlying assumption is that the person performs within the boundaries of the organizations culture. If not, as discussed before, the person is deemed not to be performing at all.

The strategy of the organization and its year-one annual business plan, once they are developed and communicated, must be fragmented and assigned to the teams which make up the organization. It is then broken down further within each team, in order to ensure its actual execution (Figure 50). The cascading of the business plan and its strategic goals or objectives follows accountability lines from top to bottom, which ensures that the achievement of the objective is within the individual's arm's reach. This takes the form of strategic initiatives or projects, which either are self-contained within a function, or become cross-functional initiatives. They find their way into the performance development system for each colleague as what we typically call vertical and horizontal strategic performance objectives. The other major or impactful objectives related to continuous improvement are typically referred to as breakthrough objectives, which is a 'Six Sigma' quality management term.

Breakthrough: An act or instance of breaking through an obstacle. A sudden advance especially in knowledge or technique

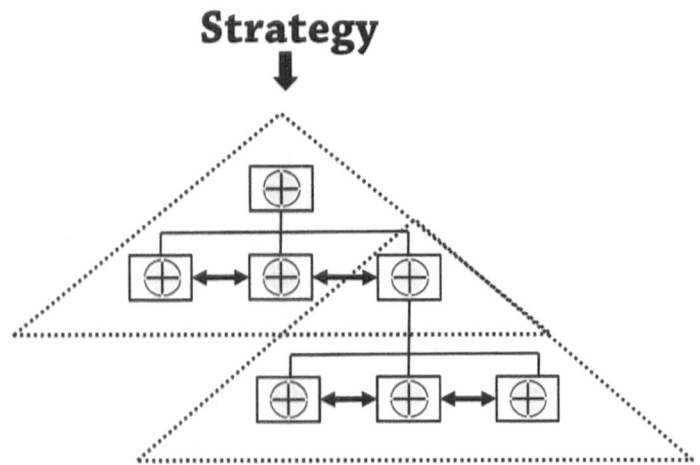

FIGURE 50 — STRATEGY ALIGNMENT

The standard framework to describe these performance objectives is called SMART (Figure 51), which has its roots in project management, and continues to be one of the best ways to avoid the setting of wishy-washy objectives for which achievement is hard to determine later. These objectives should stretch both the organization and the individual's performance. They cannot be achieved by simple, incremental, or small improvements but require individuals to extend themselves and reach for radical achievements.

Radical:	Very different from the usual or traditional. Very new and different from what is traditional or ordinary

Specific (W4 & How)
Measurable
Achievable
Relevant
Time-based (When)

FIGURE 51 — SMART GOAL-SETTING MODEL

There is another interesting goal-setting approach, which I only recently came across, called the GROW model, developed by British executive coach Graham Alexander. The model has been used extensively in Europe by Alexander (Figure 52).

Goal
Reality
Options
Will

FIGURE 52 — GROW GOAL-SETTING MODEL

It goes without saying that the execution of these objectives and the fulfilment of role accountabilities should be monitored more frequently than on an annual basis. In fact it can happen every day in conversations between a team member and their team leader. It only makes sense to synchronize these reviews with the organization's standard quarterly financial performance reviews when clear performance indicators are produced.

The documentation of these interactions, which should be in the form of factual and candid two-way conversations, should take place as often as necessary so that both parties remember, when time comes to formally review the colleague's performance, what was said and agreed upon during the year. That formal review typically occurs at the end of the fiscal year. It is wrong to wait an entire quarter to provide feedback and coaching to individuals so they perform better, or in order to correct counter-cultural and inappropriate behaviours. Professional athletes get coaching as soon as they get to the bench, not after the game or season.

Too many HR practitioners and employment lawyers try to justify the need to document performance—or the lack thereof—for the purpose of defending a potential wrongful dismissal lawsuit. The real bang-for-the-process buck is to make sure the business plan gets executed according to plan and commitments, and that colleagues get the feedback and development necessary to perform better. It is certainly useful to jot down notes or keep documents with tangible information and examples to be used as memory refreshers during a performance conversation. It also prevents the most recent performance event from tainting the entire year's performance.

In many instances, the likelihood of winning the case is minimal, as it is not only the documentation that is missing, but the whole performance feedback process itself. The performance system is rarely broken, but the team leader—sometimes the entire organization—often does not support the notion of performance feedback (*We should wonder why the team leader or organization failed so miserably*).

The infamous 'probation period' is too often used by organizations to terminate a colleague's employment without having had to document or justify any of it, and without incurring severance costs. Why would anyone agree to leave their job to join an organization, knowing that at any point during the first three or six months of tenure they can be fired without any justification or financial support to search for other employment? Personally, I would question the judgement of someone who agrees to this in the first place. It is also not a great indicator of how effective the recruitment and screening machine is if we need to give ourselves six months to figure out if we hired the right person!

I once told a prospective employer that I would certainly agree to a six-month probation period, but only if they reciprocally agreed to allow me the same period of time to determine if I had made the right choice and would provide me with the necessary severance to find alternative employment if I determined I had not—They dropped the probation clause.

There is no way out of having to complete the proverbial performance review at the end of the year. Many will argue that each individual's performance should be reviewed on some hiring anniversary date to avoid having performance reviews conducted en masse at one point during the fiscal year. The grave fallacy around this idea is that the performance objectives are tied to the fiscal year and its cycle, so to arbitrarily disconnect it would be to disassociate the execution of the business plan by teams and colleagues from the business plan itself. The solution is for HR to make the process and program effective, painless, and valuable to team leaders (*And depart from the 12-page performance review and essay-writing that goes along with it*).

During the candid conversations regarding a colleague's performance, in the context of the fulfilment of role accountabilities and the execution of strategic and breakthrough objectives, developmental needs are inevitably identified. The plan of action to address this development is aimed at enhancing the individual's performance of their current role. The longer-range development, which is often referred to as a career development plan, is aimed at getting the person ready for their next role or career advancement. These conversations occur within the same time frame and context, and they all form part of the individual's performance and career development. Most systems will require the performance reviewer to assign a specific performance rating or factor to an individual's performance, which is often perceived to be the punchline. Unfortunately, it focuses the attention of the colleague away from a valuable discussion regarding performance development to the rating.

There is an existing lobby of SMEs who suggest that those ratings should be eliminated in favour of a dialogue and statement (Figure 53). That is because, traditionally, the team leader assigns the rating in some relatively arbitrary fashion, and the performance development process is totally skewed towards the punchline rating. Some organizations even dictate the distribution of performance ratings to a pre-determined performance rating distribution curve. Of course, colleagues immediately perceive, and rightfully so, that approach as being unfair and unrelated to their actual performance.

7-Point	6-Point	5-Point	4-Point	3-Point
1. Exceptional	1. Exceptional Achievement	1. Exceptional Contributor	1. Exceptionally Successful	1. Exceeds Expectations
2. Excellent	2. Excellent Achievement	2. Superior Contributor	2. Very Successful	2. Meets Expectations
3. Very Good	3. Very Good Achievement	3. Valued Contributor	3. Relatively Successful	3. Does Not Meet Expectations
4. Good	4. Satisfactory Achievement	4. Improving Contributor	4. Marginally Successful	
5. Satisfactory	5. Adequate Achievement	5. Marginal Contributor		
6. Adequate	6. Marginal Achievement			
7. Marginal				

FIGURE 53 — PERFORMANCE RATING SCALES

That issue is far less prevalent in competency-based position profiling and performance development, for each of the role competencies can be assessed by the team leader using a list of standard behavioural statements describing proficiency levels. The SMART objectives can also be assessed fairly objectively and factually, for they are stated in a specific way. The team leader simply has to determine if the objective was under, fully, or over achieved. All of the proficiency and objective-achievement ratings are numeric, can be relatively weighted, and therefore can generate a mathematical performance rating made up of several factors, encompassing what was achieved, and how it was achieved. Some organizations even apply a difficulty or a context factor to the performance rating to recognize that not all objectives carry the same challenges, and that the business environment may have also hampered the achievement of a goal (*This 'difficulty factor' approach is also used in the Olympic Games*).

The important fact to remember is that performance development is about assessing and developing the performance of an individual against the expectations of the role they are fulfilling, and for someone paid at that level, and not relative to other individuals in the organization. How could we possibly determine the relative ranking of tens of thousands of colleagues in a global organization, who don't perform the same role, live continents apart, and are led by thousands of different leaders?

To go even further into imaginary logic, the famed CEO of General Electric, Jack Welch instituted the 'rank and yank' forced-ranking performance system, by which the bottom 10 percent of all colleagues would be fired each year. The widely held fallacy at the time was that this contributed to GE's success—from what we know now, the resulting disengagement of colleagues probably meant that GE did not do as well as it should have, had it implemented a healthy performance-development program. Other admiring CEO's adopted the practice and soon found themselves at the losing end of class-action lawsuits and created cultures where being better than the teammate, either by being better or making them look worse, would mean job security (*The best way to escape from the bear who's chasing you is not to be fast...just faster that the person you are running with*).

I am a big fan of using a four-point scale and quartile distribution to assign performance ratings (Figure 54), for it echoes what compensation SMEs use to define how the organization should pay relative to its reference employment market. It also mirrors what investors use to determine their performance relative to others in the market. The top quartile performers are deemed to be the top performers and should be rewarded accordingly.

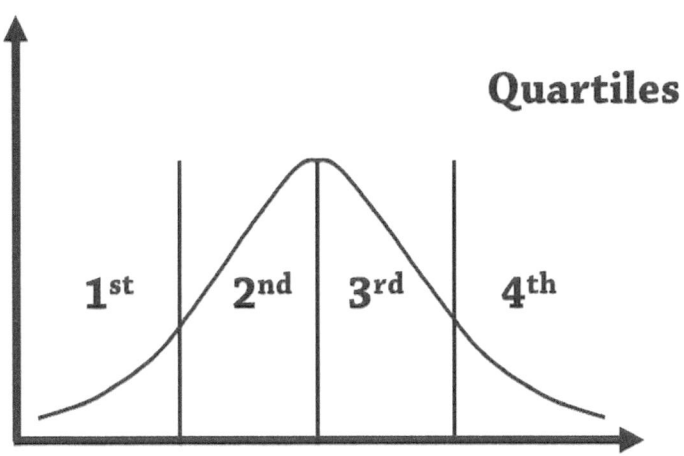

FIGURE 54 — DATA DISTRIBUTION QUARTILES

The other option is to arbitrarily cluster two sigma's at each end of the bell curve and use each of the two sigma's up and down the median to make up a four-point scale (Figure 55). The difference, using that approach, is that the top segment of performers represents 15.75 percent of the population versus 25 percent using the quartile approach. In a high-performance organization, one could assume that the bell curve would be skewed to the right, therefore increasing the percentage of high performers, which would support using the quartile rather than the sigma approach.

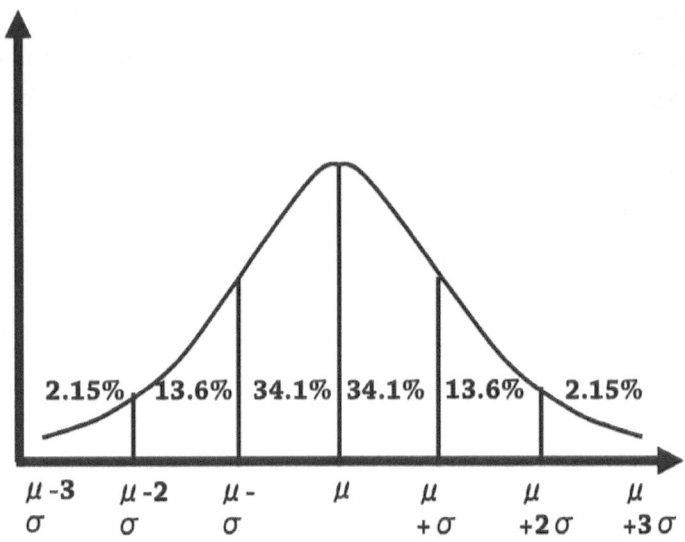

FIGURE 55 — NORMAL DISTRIBUTION CURVE

The added value of a four-point performance scale is that it forces those providing performance feedback to choose between above and below average—or median—as opposed to selecting the safer average rating (*Or sitting on the fence*).

Those ratings are required because they feed into the talent-planning grid, the salary-adjustment matrix, and the bonus-payout table. In the end, performance development will always be somewhat subjective. The trick is to remove as much subjectivity as possible and to make sure the transparency, fairness, and design of the program are re-assuring to those who take part in the process (*Or who feel subjected to it, if they believe the rating process is flawed and unfair*).

There is a way to provide even more fairness through the performance development process, which is to let more than one person provide input to a colleague's performance development. This multi-rater approach is called a 360-degree performance input, where feedback is provided by people all around the individual (Figure 56). Colleagues—including the individuals themselves—are asked to provide confidential input on a variety of factors, typically focusing on competencies (functional, managerial, & leadership) as well as core values alignment. The individual and his team leader review the results and compare it to the individual's self-assessment to look for clues related to performance (*The sad reality of 360s is that they are necessary only because of the inability of colleagues to give each other candid and constructive feedback. They resort to doing so to avoid having to confront the individual*).

The initial results debrief to the individual is typically provided by an executive coach or performance coach who is also an independent and competent third party and can help the individual in understanding their behaviours and take corrective and enhancement actions. Beware of the rapidly growing coaching industry and its most passionate apostles, for they are tempted to want to resolve any issue using coaching. It is a classic case of Maslow's Law of the Instrument: "It is tempting, if the only tool you have is a hammer, to treat everything as if it were a nail". Too many of them lack the organizational dynamics experience and associated credibility to be significantly impactful as coaches.

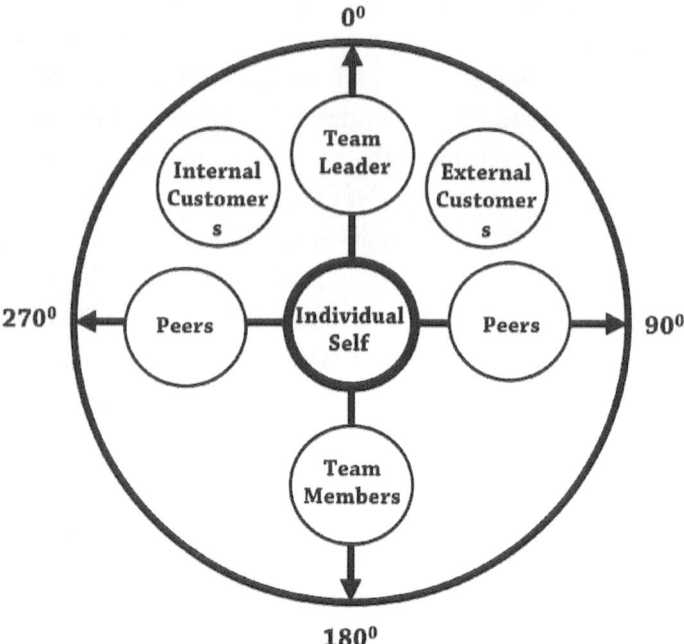

FIGURE 56 – 360° PERFORMANCE FEEDBACK

There are those who argue that 360°s should never be part of performance development, but rather only personal development. While the opinions expressed should be considered as perceptions rather than facts, and therefore not 'hardwired' to the performance system as being factual, they have to be used by the team leader as clues or hints of performance, which should be explored and investigated with those who provided input. It would be unfair to ask colleagues to complete the 360-degree questionnaire without committing that corrective action will be taken. The tool is great at helping to discover—or rather expose—individuals who have mastered the art of behaving appropriately with their team leader or senior management, but not with others. Defective leaders always behave worse with those over whom they have authority—their team members, and the receptionist (*Or the waiter*).

The actual compensation impact of performance assessment should definitely be disconnected from the performance and developmental conversations, for they tend to cloud the dialogue about the person's role, developmental needs, and ambitions. The performance conversation as you might expect becomes about money.

The leading-edge systems are transparent, simple, user friendly and technology supported. They are also directly connected to the organization's core values. The best systems have a cultural factor, or multiplier, which adjusts the numerical value of the performance rating. Unacceptable behaviours, and their correlation to any one of the core values negatively impact the cultural factor, which in turn can ultimately multiply the overall performance rating by zero, consequently freezing both salary increase and bonus payment. Such an occurrence would effectively put an incumbent's employment at risk altogether and result in the development of a short-term performance improvement plan. This is what we mean by 'hardwiring' the soft cultural stuff. These systems are fully integrated so that they feed the talent plans and affect the likelihood of career advancement accordingly.

When designed properly, the program is perceived to be invaluable by colleagues (*Unless the individual is not performing, or is a cultural misfit*) for connecting their contribution to the organization's success and its financial rewards, for providing development and career advancement, and ensuring that behaviours are compliant with the organization's core values. The system rewards the performance of role accountabilities and execution of vertical and horizontal team objectives through salary increases and the payment of performance bonuses.

TOTAL REWARDS MANAGEMENT—REWARDING PEOPLE AND TEAMS FOR EXECUTING

The topic of total compensation or rewards management, particularly for executives, cabinet ministers, athletes, performers, and civil servants is always a good one to start a heated debate at the local Starbucks or Tim Horton's (*Canada's best* ☺) over a cup of coffee and a local newspaper. Citizens of the world are fascinated with the money, perks, and lavish lifestyles of the rich and famous. We also complain about them keeping their jobs, or getting big bonuses regardless of their performance—the athlete hasn't scored, the company lost money, the country is in a recession, or the movie is terrible. Of course, by most of our standards, these people are obscenely and grossly overpaid.

That feeling is anchored in our collective misconception and ignorance of what is appropriate or not in terms of compensation. This springs from a lack of knowledge of reference points, and by the fact that, somewhere along the economic food chain, someone agreed to pay these people that much. We don't even know what life is like for these regal few, or what it took them to get there. Really, most of us just don't know what we are talking about (*Or are simply envious*). The whole compensation thing is misunderstood and mistrusted by colleagues because of its opacity. That is why the best thing to do is educate everyone as to how it works, and make sure the program is simple.

We historically kept compensation in a shroud of secrecy and opacity out of concern for the confidentiality of information and respect for the privacy of individual recipients—and often because the system is indeed arbitrary and inequitable. However, the regulations requiring the disclosure of publicly-traded companies' top executives have provided a glimpse to all of us commoners. The internet provides free and relatively reliable data on salaries. Government departments, because of the inherent need for public disclosure, have long had the practice of publishing salary ranges, and even salaries of top civil servants.

All of this information provides for dangerous speculation about how the rest of them are compensated, and how each of us fared in comparison. The issue of pay continues to be in the top five attraction and retention drivers, according to the Towers Watson 2012 Global Workforce Study. The only practical way for organizations to appease individual's engagement concerns is by educating them about the system and process and by being transparent about the compensation structure.

The socialists amongst us like to use the average salary of a CEO as a multiple of the average salary of the rank and file employee. Peter Drucker believed it was morally and socially unforgivable for that ratio to be more than 20x. In fact, the Obama administration's Dodd–Frank Wall Street Reform and Consumer Protection Act—enacted as a result of the 2007 Wall Street collapse—will soon require publicly-traded organizations to disclose such a multiple. While most industry analysts believe that the multiple is on average between 30x to 40x, a 2010 white paper by Radford Consulting showed that that multiple could be as high as 78x.

The government reassures us that such disasters will never happen again thanks to these massive measures. But as is so often the case, these measures are only ever enacted after the disasters have already occurred, following months—if not years—of bells and whistles going off. We now have to comply with the Sarbanes-Oxley Act so that Enron doesn't happen again. We get our shoes scanned and shampoo seized at the airport to prevent some fanatic from high jacking or blowing up the aircraft. And now comes Dodd-Frank, so that the greedy Wall Street and financial types don't bring down the economy again (*What is it with these people?*). The tragedy is that by all accounts, none of these measures would have prevented the crises that they are designed to prevent in the first place. There were ample warning signs that were just ignored. We are all victims of governments giving us emotional and psychological comfort so that we quickly go about our lives and refuel the economy, and then their re-election, so that business resumes as usual. It is scary how we have become so accustomed to being fooled (*It's the 'drive-thru phenomenon' which Leo Getz vividly described in Lethal Weapon 2*).

I continue to be fascinated by the fact that legislators will compel publicly-traded organizations to adopt these onerous measures to reassure investors (*The same Capital Street types*) that these perverse executive compensation packages will no longer be offered. Aren't members of a Board of Directors appointed to represent the interests of shareholders and accountable to do so in the first place? Should they not seek advice from reputable and independent compensation consultants as opposed to relying on executive recruitment firms?

The sad reality is that many Directors are senior executives themselves, who have benefited from these schemes, and don't see anything wrong with them. You may argue that this phenomenon only applies to the CEO but that the rest of the compensation program is sound. This is simply not the case, for the CEO's compensation is typically structured and aligned to the C-level executive team, which flows through in an aligned way down the organization's structure. Any CHRO is in a conflict of interest position in recommending the CEO's compensation to the Board of Directors. I have argued that point with many heads of the HR & Compensation Committee of the Board.

The question of what is the job worth, either for a CEO or any other role, cannot simplistically be derived as a multiple of what the rank and file employee earns, any more than how much more Tom Hanks or Jodie Foster get paid for a movie relative to the cameramen. The price to be paid for a role, as any other commodity or service, is a function of offer and demand on the employment market. If some people are crazy enough to pay $4,000 for a Louis Vuitton handbag or $160,000 for a 1787 Chateau Lafite bottle of wine, so are some Board of Directors who are willing to pay $12 Million in cash compensation, excluding stock and options, to the under-performing CEO. This number is actually much higher if the CEO happens to be the founder or controlling shareholder (*Surprised?*). That is because the market dictates it.

What do Phil Mickelson, LeBron James, David Beckham, and Kobe Bryant have in common? They were each paid $40 million plus in 2010, and that is because we all agreed to pay that amount of money for the game tickets and merchandise, and agreed to suffer through countless commercials during game broadcasts. These businesses could therefore afford, and considered it to be a wise investment, to pay them that much. As long as investors continue to buy the corporation's stock, the phenomenon will persist.

There is a reason why, over the past decade or so, we have changed the terminology from compensation to rewards. We finally decided to adjust the terminology to reflect the true intent and meaning of the word. The idea of simply compensating someone for doing a job lacks the notion of correlating how well the job is done with how much is paid for it. What organizations pay for is output and the achievement of committed-upon objectives. The successful values-driven organizations, as we discussed earlier, will also embed the concept of how the job is performed, and not simply what is achieved when it comes to rewarding and recognizing performance. The term total rewards now encompasses each of the rewards elements an incumbent receives in return for their short and long-term contribution.

With the world becoming flatter and flatter (*Check out 'The World Is Flat: A Brief History of the Twenty-First Century'*[27] *by Thomas Friedman*), the imperatives of global competitiveness are more pressing than ever. It does not matter where you are in the world now; someone on any of the other continents is competing for your business. That is putting pressure on productivity, which unfortunately is often interpreted by uncreative business leaders to mean that compensation has to be frozen or reduced, and that jobs have to be eliminated. The short-sighted flaw of that approach is that, for most organizations, people costs don't represent that great of a proportion of all costs and that what really matters is productivity. What matters is having the most output with the least cost, which means that to have three great people earning $100K who produce more output faster than five of them being paid $75K each is better.

The compensation attached to any role has multiple components (Figure 57), each of which is determined using total compensation market surveys provided by independent professional services firms. The surveys are assembled by asking participants to provide information about their particular compensation. The sample of participants should really be made up of those employers where the organization is likely to either attract from or lose its colleagues to—the reference employment market.

- Fixed Compensation (base salary)
- Variable Compensation (bonus, incentive, commission)
- Long-term Incentive Compensation (stock options)
- Perquisite Compensation (perks)
- Benefits:
  - Retirement
  - Health
  - Insurance (life & disability)
  - Vacation, Statutory Holidays
- Intangibles (subsidies, development, amenities)

FIGURE 57 — TOTAL COMPENSATION ELEMENTS

The surveys typically define role mandates, which companies attempt to match to their own set of roles. There exists a wide variation of mandates and role accountabilities in the samples, which is why compensation is not a science, let alone a precise one. The illusion of scientific precision is created by expressing the market value of a position to the last dollar. The results of these surveys are collated and provided back to the group of participants. The results for each surveyed role will typically be segmented by industry, size of company (revenues and number of employees), and geography. Each of the total compensation elements is shown in percentile or quartile and median of the survey group sampled. An organization is then able to determine how much a role is worth in the employment market, and the level of each compensation element.

The next step is to decide how the organization wants to position itself relative to the survey data. The compensation policy will determine how the organization pays relative to which quartile of the market, for which family of roles, and for which element of the total compensation. Most organizations now choose to position themselves at the median of the market for most families of roles. They may, for example, choose the third quartile position for a family of roles which is in high demand and likely to suffer turnover or delayed talent acquisition. In some cases, the organization will arbitrarily select one component of the total compensation program, such as health or retirement benefits, and peg it at the third or fourth quartile to brand or differentiate its culture as a caring one.

The total rewards structure defines what grade or band, which compensation elements, and which hierarchic title is attached to which role in the organization. The structure is only a tool designed to ensure market competitiveness and internal equity within the organization. It is as much of a guide as a financial budget is. There are typically 15 to 25 overlapping ranges or grades (Figure 58) in the structure, with the Chief Executive being the highest. The width of each range, defined as the minimum and maximum, is typically set at +/- 20 percent of the range's midpoint or market median.

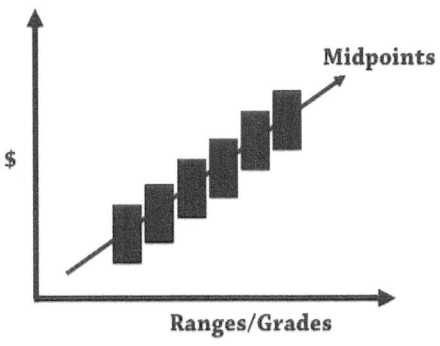

FIGURE 58 — RANGE STRUCTURE ILLUSTRATION

In recent years, broad bands comprising of several grades were introduced to enhance the width of the ranges and provide more flexibility (Figure 59) when determining an incumbent's base salary.

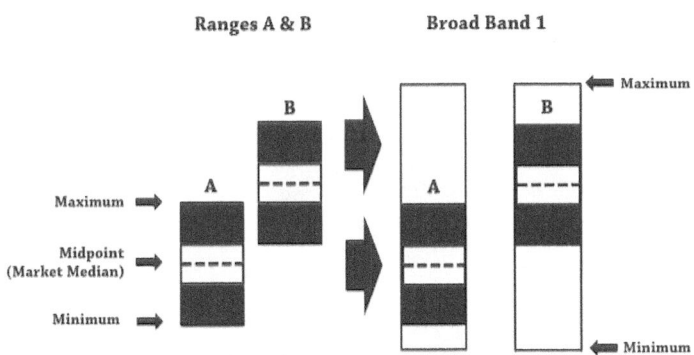

FIGURE 59 — COMPENSATION RANGES
INSERTION INTO BROAD BANDS

There are many ways to evaluate roles, going from a fully subjective determination to a near scientific one. Some organizations still insist on using job evaluation systems called Point Factor Analysis (PFA), where each aspect of a job is rated, weighted and then allocated a total number of points (Figure 60). These systems became very popular because of the enactment of various pay-equity legislations requiring an organization to confirm equity amongst roles by assessing the skill, effort, responsibility, and working conditions requirements. Labor unions also insisted in inserting the concept into collective agreements.

Accountability
    Freedom to Act
    Scope
    Impact

Know-How
    Technical/Specialized Skills
    Managerial Skills
    Human Relations Skills

Problem Solving
    Thinking Environment
    Thinking Challenge

Source: HayGroup®

FIGURE 60 — JOB EVALUATION DIMENSIONS AND FACTORS

The jobs with similar points are then assigned to the same job grade. By correlating the evaluations with how much the employment market pays, it essentially allocates an amount of compensation pay per point (*admittedly I am being overly simplistic here*). The use of these systems gives the illusion of precision in job evaluation and creates this incredibly rigid committee-driven bureaucracy and culture of empire building necessary to justify more points, higher grades, and more compensation. Those most gifted in writing these job descriptions—using the right adverbs and adjectives—can push the evaluations up the scale. In a dynamic environment, which is the norm nowadays, incumbents continually ask for their roles to be re-evaluated as role parameters change.

While the factors being assessed are certainly aligned to effective role profiling and are also supportive of the Accountabilities & Authorities approach, the subjectivity applied by a committee while evaluating each factor and dimension, combined with the inherent margin of error contained in compensation surveys, do not justify the effort needed to manage such programs. These PFA systems should be used by compensation SMEs only as a means of validating or auditing fully subjective job evaluations and complying with pay equity legislation.

The value of a role out there in the employment market, and its relative value to other roles, is determined by the market itself. The employment market naturally determines what roles are worth the same compensation. Using job evaluation is very similar to conducting a professional property appraisal to assign a market value to a real estate property, rather than asking a real estate agent for an opinion. Ultimately, the actual value of the property is always determined by the market, which is to say what a buyer is prepared to pay. The organization's internal recruiters can act as effective 'compensation agents' as they gather valuable employment market compensation data during interviews.

Asking a reputable recruitment consultant for their opinion on the value of the role is also quite reliable, as they too are gaining even better market-pricing intelligence through the interviewing of candidates not only for multiple jobs, but also many organizations. The price of each role fluctuates and is determined by the market. Internally, the organization is prepared to pay the price, providing that the role is fully performed as measured by output. What matters is that the role-evaluation process and outcomes are transparent, simple, easily defended, and supportive of internal equity and market competitiveness. The performance-development systems ensure that the organization gets appropriate value from the role through the incumbent's output.

The output of each role, and intrinsically its incumbent, is determined by using the performance development program and process. The fulfilment of role accountabilities and the achievement of SMART breakthrough and strategic objectives are discussed and assessed. Each key accountability is rated, a proficiency level is assigned to each competency, and each objective is assigned an achievement rating. The overall performance of the incumbent is then determined by the team leader, who assigns a performance rating.

The overall performance rating is entered into a base salary increase matrix (Figure 61) and provides the team leader with a range of potential salary increases which can be awarded to the incumbent. The matrix is designed to reward performance, as it will provide the highest increase to a colleague who is paid the least and performs the best relative to expectations and provides no increase to someone who is highly paid but not performing well. It stands to reason that the higher a person is paid, the higher their performance expectations should be.

Performance Factor	Compa-Ratio (%)											
	80 - 89			90 - 99			100 - 109			110 - 119			120+		
	min	mid	max	min	mid	max	min	mid	max	min	mid	max	min	mid	max
Exceeds	80%	CPI+7	120%	80%	CPI+5	120%	80%	CPI+3	120%	80%	CPI+1	120%	80%	CPI	120%
Meets	80%	CPI+5	120%	80%	CPI+3	120%	80%	CPI+1	120%	80%	CPI	120%			
Partially Meets	80%	CPI+3	120%	80%	CPI+1	120%	80%	CPI	120%						
Does Not Meet															

FIGURE 61 — CONSUMER PRICE INDEX-BASED
ANNUAL SALARY INCREASE MATRIX

As a rule of thumb, it should not take more than three to four years for a high performer to reach the midpoint, or market rate, of the compensation range, if they started at the bottom of it at an entry-level salary. Assuming that there is a 20 percent gap between the bottom of each range and the midpoint (See Figure 59), a high performer's salary should move up at a net five-seven percent per year. The range's midpoint typically moves with CPI every year, hence the attention to net salary increases. The matrix is designed to make sure performers who are paid at the market rate receive the employment market increase thus maintaining their standard of living.

The Employment Market Adjustment (EMA) is based on CPI but can be higher if the market is heating up due to a low unemployment rate and demand for talent. The reverse is true as well. It is also risky for an organization, where workforce cost makes up a large proportion of their product or service cost, to be impacted by the compounded effect of consecutive increases in salary if the price of their product is not increasing at the same rate.

The concept is also very much used by labour unions when signing multi-year collective agreements, whereby pay scales, and consequently every worker's salary, is automatically adjusted by a Cost Of Living Allowance (COLA), calculated using CPI. These adjustments are typically universal, and not related to an individual's performance. Governments generally adjust social security and minimum wages using CPI as well.

The incumbents should strive to be promoted out of their current role and into a higher compensation grade, where their new compensation will be lower relative to the new range and therefore subject to higher salary increases upon performance. Conversely, the matrix design will prevent a low performer from receiving a salary increase. The comparison ration, or 'compa-ratio' as it is commonly known, is an individual's current salary expressed as a percentage of the midpoint or market rate. An individual whose compa-ratio is high, but with only adequate performance, will receive a low salary increase as the individual would have reached that level of compa-ratio through high performance, but is now 'coasting'. As I indicated earlier, it is imperative that performance be evaluated against expectations relative to where the colleague's compensation is pegged within the range as opposed to the full-fledged expectations of a role, where midpoint compensation would be paid. This will avoid assigning automatic 'needs development' or 'does not meet expectations' ratings to a high performer who has just been promoted into a new role, something which does not do well for a colleague's engagement.

Each team leader has a salary increase budget assigned for their team. Once all of the performance ratings are entered, the team leader will tweak the salary increases and distribute the salary increase budget amongst their team. The aggregate salary increase budget has historically been determined using various economic projections and surveys provided by compensation consulting firms, governments, and think tanks. Those are normally the object of weeks of analysis and presentation to the leadership of the organization and the HR or compensation committee of the Board. After years of agony and frustration over this crazy process, a former team member and Total Rewards SME pointed out that the number always ends up being approximately CPI, plus the one or two percentage points necessary to allow for adequate salary progression (*Precise enough for me!*).

The increases of base salary are often perceived by colleagues to be small in comparison to the potential payment of bonuses or variable compensation. However, the net present value of increasing base salaries by only a few percentage points is very high and remains within the cost base of the organization, regardless of its performance. That is why most organizations would rather pay lower salaries and offer higher bonuses. Those bonuses effectively become 're-earnable' base salary when repeatedly paid as a result of sustained performance (*And you thought only George W. Bush and Alexander Haig could come up with such inventive terminology!*).

Short-Term Variable Compensation (Bonus)

There is an age-old argument in the HR world regarding what the variable compensation, bonus, incentive, or commission schemes should be called – either incentive or reward programs. As a self-confessed terminology freak, it is important to point out that what we call incentive programs or compensation is not, in itself, what actually motivates individuals to behave in one way or another, to perform or not.

It can also be argued that the payment of base salary is a reward for adequately performing a role. The difference is that the payment of a base salary, or not, is a binary proposition and translates to termination of employment (*The zero option*) rather than the progressive payment of variable cash rewards. Most individuals would respond well without having financial rewards associated with either the behaviours or objectives. The payment of bonuses is a tangible reward for having done so. Personal or public recognition is also a reward, granted intangible.

I have worked with colleagues who were convinced that the entire organization could be self-lead or governed by an appropriate and comprehensive variable-compensation program. Colleagues would behave the right way and achieve performance objectives, as described in the variable compensation program document. The leadership of the team would actually be delegated to the incentive compensation program. That is what poor leaders *(Or mercenaries)* believe and advocate.

Incentive:	Something that incites or has a tendency to incite to determination or action. Something that encourages a person to do something or to work harder
Incite:	To move to action, stir up, spur on, urge on

Reward:	To give money or another kind of payment to someone or something for something good that has been done
Recognition:	Special attention or notice especially by the public for someone's work or actions

Variable compensation is designed to adjust the individual's compensation based on performance. The pay-for-performance approach works for base or fixed compensation as well, but the bigger performance bang for payment buck is incontestably with variable compensation. Another term used for variable compensation is 'at risk' i.e. at risk of not being paid if not performing. As one can imagine, risk-taking shareholders love to see senior executives, and ideally every colleague, being in the risk boat along with them. In most cases, the risk/benefit equation for variable compensation schemes works this way: the risk of not getting paid is offset by a very attractive payout potential for high performance (*The stock market works the same way: the higher the risk, the higher the potential reward*).

Most of us are familiar with commission sales programs, where the sales person gets paid a percentage of what they sell or a set amount for each unit sold. These individuals typically get no base salary, unless they are paid an advance on future commissions called a draw. The risk of non-performance is therefore fully absorbed by the incumbent. It is not uncommon for organizations to either have their own sales force, or use local agents and distributors to represent them. The cost of sales is either calculated as a percentage of products sold by either the agent or by an internal salesperson. Here are a couple of reasonable questions: Who in their right mind would accept 100 percent of the risk of performing or not? What kind of behaviours do these programs encourage? And why is it that commission programs are always in sales?

If there is one thing I learned in the sales compensation world, it is that sales incentives should never be paid as a function of sale revenues if the individual sales person recommends or decides on the price. In that case, the incentive should be paid on the amount of gross margin dollars generated by the sale, which rewards selling at the highest price possible without losing the sale. In the end, the program design should always be about which behaviour we want to reward.

Variable compensation programs are designed to reward individuals and teams for the achievement of team and individual performance objectives, while respecting the organization's core values. The achievement of objectives, if stated in a SMART way, can be effectively determined using reliable measurements and metrics (*The 'M' in SMART*). The variable compensation target is generally expressed as a percentage of an individual's base salary, which is also how compensation surveys express it. The target is what gets paid when the 'stretch' or ambitious performance objectives are achieved. This should not be confused with profit-sharing plans, which simply distribute a set portion of the organization's profit to employees at year-end. There is very little reward value to these programs, as there is no visible cause-and-effect relationship between a colleague and the organization's profitability (*It might as well be a Christmas gift*).

In an ideal world, the variable compensation program generates the right employment market quartile total cash compensation for the equivalent product market performance—translation: if the organization performs at the fourth quartile of its industry or market, its colleagues should be compensated at the fourth quartile of its reference employment market. Shareholders criticize boards of Directors when the compensation paid to its senior executives is neither aligned nor reflective of the organization's performance. The price of the stock is rarely the issue, as shareholders realize how emotional and volatile stock markets are. They typically focus on other measures such as growth, profitability, and market share.

For purely numeric objectives, such as sales, revenues, market share, units produced, customer satisfaction, or colleague engagement, a payout curve is designed. The curve shows what percentage of the variable target compensation will be paid when achieving what percentage of the performance target (Figure 62). The slope of the payout curves is decided upon by determining the appropriate cost of incremental variable payment for incremental achievement. The threshold is the minimum performance required for any payout to be made, with the target being the agreed-upon level of performance or achievement. The slope of the payout curve will typically increase gradually to provide a further reward to the individuals who over-achieve. I like to use the analogy of hurdle sprinters who try to reach an imaginary finish line, which is a few meters past the actual line in order to avoid the tendency to slow down before crossing the line.

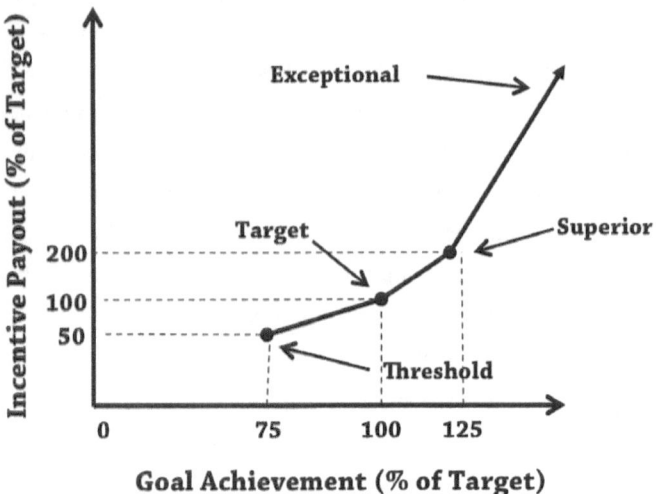

FIGURE 62 — PAYMENT OF INCENTIVE
RELATIVE TO PERFORMANCE

One of the best ways to design these programs, other than asking specialized consultants, is for HR to partner with the Finance team and then test the preliminary designs with a focus group of top performers (*Never ask for volunteers, you may get the whiners*). This approach was confirmed in the results of a June 2010 survey conducted by Loyola University, the Hay Group, and the World-at-Work total rewards association. Shareholders are willing to invest variable compensation dollars to generate incremental net income above target, providing colleagues are prepared to invest significant incremental effort.

The performance objectives assigned to an individual need to be relatively weighted, as different objectives will undoubtedly be more or less impactful and complex and some will require more time and effort to complete than others. The target variable component is then broken down and attached to respective objectives, based on their weight. Most organizations will dictate which of the relative portion of the variable target is to be allocated to which category of objective. The mix is determined by the role position within the hierarchy (Figure 63), and governed by the within arm's reach concept. This means that individuals should only be rewarded for performance outcomes they impact. *(And I did not say control the outcome).*

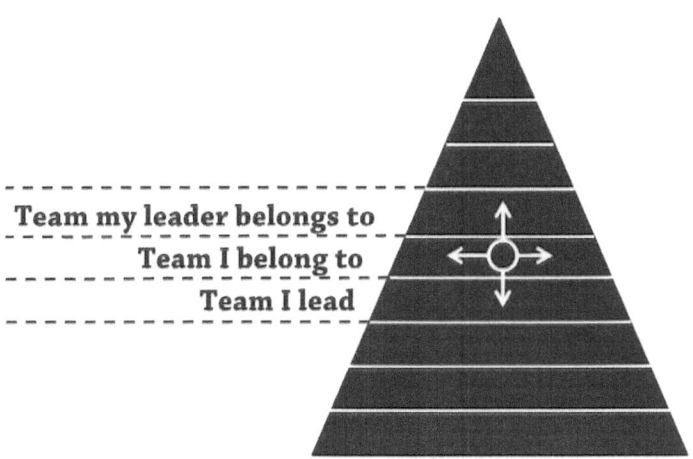

FIGURE 63 — ROLE ARM'S REACH WITHIN HIERARCHY

Each individual should have a portion of their incentive target assigned to both their vertical and horizontal teams' performance objectives so as to reward cooperation and contribution to both and to encourage a balanced perspective (Figure 64). We typically deem that the reach is up to the team an individual's team leader belongs to, or one level above.

Component	% of Incentive Target	Goals	% of Component
One Above	20	Goal A	70
		Goal B	30
		Total	100
Horizontal	30	Goal A	10
		Goal B	90
		Total	100
Vertical	50	Goal A	20
		Goal B	35
		Goal C	45
		Total	100
Total	100		

FIGURE 64 — ILLUSTRATIVE INCENTIVE STRUCTURE

There is a practice amongst leading high-performance organizations of not allowing for the payment of any bonus to an individual who is deemed to be an unsuccessful performer. Also, no payment of the horizontal team component of the bonus is made to an individual unless the vertical team they lead has reached a minimum threshold. This supports the notion that, in order to benefit from the success of my horizontal team, I have to have contributed to its success by effectively leading my vertical team.

The variable compensation programs for the sales or revenue-generation machine are traditionally more risky than those of other functions, with a larger proportion of the total cash at target compensation being allocated to the variable component. (*It is 100 percent for pure commission sales teams*). This phenomenon is also true as the roles gain altitude within the organization's hierarchy. The logic being that the Chief Executive Officer has far more authority and impact on the performance of the organization than the front-line colleague. *(I cringe when ill-informed backbenchers object to executives having large variable compensation targets—in reality, it means that a substantial portion of their compensation is at risk of not being paid at all).*

The variable compensation program is connected to published indicators or metrics, which are reflective of the business' performance. These Key Performance Indicators (KPIs) are normally those needed to determine if strategic objectives and the business plan are being achieved as planned and committed to. Each of these KPIs is included in a performance dashboard or balanced scorecard. The organization typically has an enterprise-level dashboard, with other functions using subsets or more granular dashboards. In order to be trusted, the dashboard's metrics and dials must be legitimate and transparent, and directly extracted from reliable, if not audited, operational and financial reporting. Robert S. Kaplan and David P. Norton published the book *The Balanced Scorecard*[28] in 1996, and popularized the concept (Figure 65).

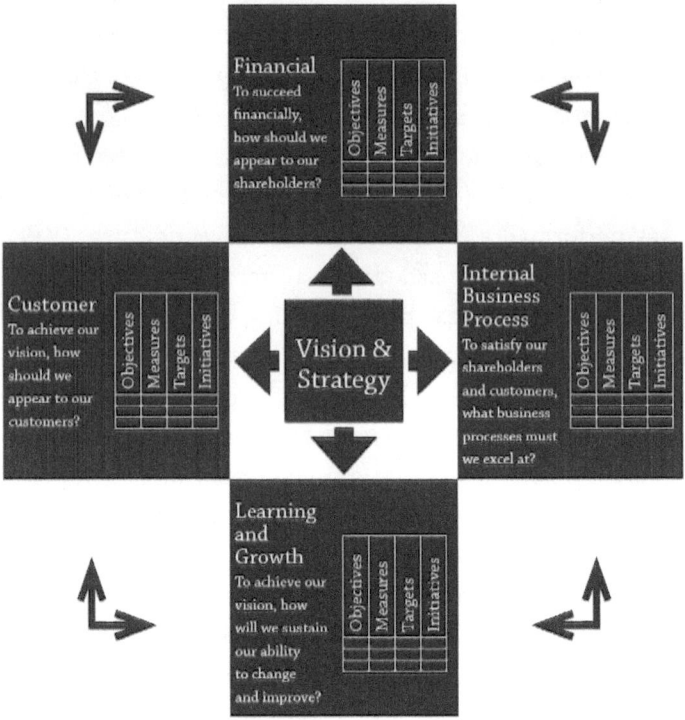

FIGURE 65 — BALANCED SCORECARD FRAMEWORK

The dashboard term is very popular now in business, but we also see some firms and software providers referring to cockpit or instrument panel, which is better reflective of the concept. Very few drivers actually refer to their vehicle's dashboard to drive it, other than the speedometer (*I learned to drive in Montreal where speeding limits are considered a suggestion only. I think discounted speeding season tickets should be available*).

Conversely, a flight crew not only has to constantly monitor the aircraft's performance, but also has to rely on instruments to navigate and execute its flight plan, particularly when flying without visibility under Instrument Flight Rules (IFR). In the organization, we execute business and strategic plans (*Same idea*).

The paramount need for Crew Resource Management (CRM) parallels nicely with the notion that metrics are required, but that leadership and teamwork onboard are what effectively achieve the mission with adequate risk management and the avoidance of catastrophic errors. The need to monitor each gauge on the instrument panel in a balanced way to assess situations and trends is also critical. A flight crew only observing low fuel consumption and rapidly increasing airspeed, without monitoring declining altitude, attitude, and ground speed could easily conclude that they are running an efficient flight as opposed to nose-diving towards the ground at an increasingly higher speed.

In the organization, the same phenomenon applies, as one cannot focus on one performance gauge only, at the detriment of others. For example, it would be like reducing customer service costs while negatively impacting customer satisfaction. The simplest and best example of that is to remember that profit can be realized in two ways, either by increasing revenues, or reducing expenses. Focusing on either variables of the equation can lead to disastrous consequences. It is too tempting to focus on cutting costs only, as the organization is in full control of those, but no one has ever been successful that way. Growth is far more difficult and risky, as it requires leadership, innovation, and customer centricity. The control of revenue growth is ultimately in the hands of the market and its customers.

It is paramount for the organization to clearly understand which of its performance indicators are 'leading' and which are 'lagging' in order to be in a position to be forward looking and adjust the course regularly and rapidly. The leading indicators are predictive of what the lagging, or trailing, indicators will eventually turn out to be (*The lagging indicators are in fact historical or rear-view mirror indicators*). Profitability and shareholder value are only lagging indicators.

According to the Royal Aeronautical Society, CRM is defined as a management system (Figure 66) which, combined with a high degree of technical knowledge, makes best use of all available resources—equipment, procedures (*Or processes*), and people—to achieve optimum efficiency in the conduct of operations while at the same time maximizing flight safety.

- Situational Awareness
- Problem Solving
- Planning and Decision Making
- Communications
- Teamwork
- Emotional Climate
- Stress Management

FIGURE 66 — CREW RESOURCE MANAGEMENT (CRM) SYSTEM ELEMENTS

Long-term Incentive (LTI) Compensation

The shareholders of either privately-held or publicly-traded organizations either have short-term or long-term goals when it comes to the return on their investments. They also want the financial interest of the organization's senior leadership to be aligned with theirs. They came up with creative ways to do so, either by paying cash, giving stock, or granting options to buy stock. Of course, they would rather use stock, as it is the primary way they realize gain on their investment, other than dividends. Some investors actually insist on members of the executive leadership team having to buy and actually own stock *(They get a real quick idea of how confident the team is in the organization's future by their willingness to invest their own money)*.

The payment of cash and stock awards is typically related to the achievement of specific financial goals over a multi-year period, either in a rolling years fashion or time elapsed from grant. The purpose is to reward senior leaders for creating sustainable value for shareholders, thus avoiding the temptation to artificially boost the price of the stock by making undesirable short-term business decisions and then pulling a 'cash and dash'.

The granting of stock options—to buy the stock in the future at today's price—is probably the most common way publicly-traded and pre-Initial Public Offering (pre-IPO) organizations choose to provide their colleagues with long-term rewards. For publicly-traded organizations, the grants are typically made yearly and their cash value, which is the number of stock multiplied by the stock price, is determined as a percentage of the recipient's annual base compensation. A portion of the granted options becomes available, or vested, to be exercised or bought over a multi-year period, and then expiring after several years if not exercised. *(The best ones adjust the grants up or down based on the combination of individual and organization performance).* Pre-IPO companies typically will express the grants of stock options as a percentage of issued common stock; the CEO for example may get four to five percent of the company's common stock. In both cases, shareholders will decide how much of the stock they are prepared to reserve for the granting of options —probably between 10 and 15 percent.

There is a lot of research and evidence to suggest (*It kind of intuitively makes sense to you and me*) that there is not much correlation between the granting of options or stock and how much value is created for shareholders. Most of us understand that great people and leaders just do what is right for the customer, the people and the business, and then the rest follows, including the stock price. Most of us rarely look at the stock price. In fact, we do not worry much about shareholders. We focus on the customer. Shareholders invest to make money and too often project themselves into what motivates the corporation's leadership. Executives want businesses to be successful, and they know the only way to get there is by exceeding the customer's expectations.

Stocks are like any other commodity, and offer and demand determine their price. Of course, the price goes up when investors believe that the stock will be in demand. That is a function of the performance of the organization but also of other unrelated industry, economic, environmental, political and social events. The stock market can be volatile, capricious, and unpredictable, but in the end, as Warren Buffett said, "If a business does well, the stock eventually follows."

The authors of an article published in the American Marketing Association's Journal of Marketing in January of 2006, entitled '*Customer Satisfaction and Stock Prices: High Returns, Low Risk*'[29], found that customer satisfaction, as measured by the American Customer Satisfaction Index (ACSI), is significantly related to market value of equity. Yet, the publication of ACSI results does not move share prices. The assumption is that customer satisfaction is a leading indicator of future market performance (*No kidding...*). That assumption is validated by further research they conducted, which showed that, between February 18, 1997, and May 21, 2003, a period when the stock market had both ups and downs, the top customer-satisfaction companies generated a cumulative return of 40 percent. It outperformed the Dow Jones Industrial Average (DJIA) by 93 percent, the S&P 500 by 201 percent, and NASDAQ by 335 percent (*How many investors, brokers and analysts understand this concept? Probably not many*).

Perquisite Compensation (Perks)

The perquisites attached to the total compensation package are known as the nice little things that come with the job. The challenge with perks is that they are visibly symbolic of hierarchy—I am more important than you, so I have an assigned parking spot in front of the building for everyone can see. There is ample evidence out there that class-consciousness is not supportive of teamwork, candour and colleague engagement. Sure, it may make the perk recipient feel good, but one should really wonder about an individual's motivation and values if they respond to symbols of superiority. I had a former colleague really upset because his office had to be relocated, with the tragic consequence of him no longer being able to see his parked Lexus. He reacted even more emotionally when he was told not to worry, as he was losing his reserved parking spot anyway. Perks make a cultural statement.

There is nothing fundamentally wrong with offering perks as they add a nice touch and some kind of emotional value to the employment proposition. In some regions, the perks are more tax effective than compensation, and therefore they also provide better value for the same cost (*Unfortunately, in most countries the government has found of way to fully tax the value of these perks*). The secret is not to link them to hierarchy, but rather logically and transparently connect them to legitimate functional requirements associated with a role.

If the role warrants frequent road travel, then maybe a vehicle should be part of the compensation package. If the role constantly requires the incumbent to hold meetings, maybe their office should be big enough to contain a conference table. If the role requires the hosting of customers and stakeholders, maybe the office furnishings should reflect the desired brand or image. Maybe only those having to use their vehicle for business on any given day or those with physical restrictions should be given the parking spots closest to the building. Maybe the abundant ambient light near the windows and views (*Most enhanced in corner offices*) should be available to those who sit at their desk all day. Maybe flying business class should be a function of frequency and length of travel, time zone differentials, and time elapsed between landing and first business event.

Thanks to technology, we have finally figured out how to offer totally flexible compensation, including perks without the historical administrative and transactional burden. This means that each colleague can customize or tailor their compensation— within reasonable limits—to their needs at any point in their career. The value of all of the elements of the package is collected into a total compensation envelope and can be used to purchase more or less of any elements. Gen X employees tend to want to buy more vacation time, for example. This way, any colleague can buy any perk that fits into the envelope.

The other option is to offer the same perks to everyone, but in varied size and cost, based on the value of the role on the market. That is what leading organizations do. Nobody would be surprised to find out that the Chief Executive makes more money than most of us, lives in a larger house, and drives a more expensive car. What people resent are status and hierarchy symbols. This is another reason why compensation should be market and function-based, transparent, and understood by colleagues.

To those vocal few *(There is always one resident social-justice apostle)* who would complain about the fact that the sales team would get a trip to the Caribbean after a great performance year I would respond, "You too can participate next year, providing you become a salesperson, bust your butt on the road chasing customers every day, and be successful. Go ahead. And by the way, you also get a company vehicle with that."

A former colleague of mine, who is now a good friend, used to drive his 15-year old Camaro to business meetings and scare customers to death when expressing his concern that the car would not start in cold weather or would not park downhill because of a leaking gas tank. So we introduced new wording on the car-allowance program specifying the age, mileage and type of vehicles allowed to be used by those with a vehicle allowance. *(I guess we realized our customer-facing colleagues' vehicles should adequately reflect the organization's image...).*

Benefits

The health benefits offered to colleagues, including life insurance and disability, have taken a much more prevalent place on most organization's radars over the past decade or so. The aging population, rising chronic disease rates, and the constant media coverage of crowded hospital emergency rooms and inflationary healthcare costs keeps the topic top of mind.

In jurisdictions where health care is government provided, benefits really means upgraded hospital stays and the reimbursement of prescription drugs and elective dental care. Where only private healthcare is available, benefits means one of the two life partners having to be employed in order to be covered. In recent past, benefits SME's and their consultants have spent a lot of energy and money educating the population about much needed changes to the health benefits package—meaning the measures having to be taken to constrain rapidly-increasing costs (*And their premiums*). Short of reducing or eliminating benefits, the most effective way to reduce their cost is by investing in prevention as a means of avoiding the health risks from materializing, and by equating the physical pain of suffering a preventable health issue with the financial pain of consuming the benefits.

It may be a novel reality, but it is actually cheaper to prevent than cure, and too many human beings do not live a healthy lifestyle. Physical health is predominantly about nutrition and physical activity (*Here is a simplistic politically-incorrect statement*). Only a small proportion of conditions are genetically related, and even those can be mitigated. For example, if there is a history of cardiovascular issues in a family, doesn't it make sense to be even more cautious about nutrition, tobacco use, and physical conditioning? In this world of rights and freedoms, each of us has the right to smoke and die prematurely (*I know, smoking is killing them slowly, but they don't care, they are not in a rush*). Now here is the problem that we non-smokers as well as premium taxpayers have with that statement—smokers consume a disproportionate amount of health care resources. Yes, we should be thankful to them for paying all of those tobacco taxes during their shorter-than-expected lifetime, but the person should also pay for the incremental healthcare costs.

Most individuals, unless they are an astronaut assigned to space station, can get out of the house and move (*The astronauts found a way to exercise by artificially reproducing gravity*). We now even found a way for couch potatoes to get fit while playing video games...It's called a Wii™. The beauty about those electronic motion-controlled video games, other than the fact that you have to get off the couch and actually move to play it, is that it makes it a challenge to maintain a normal consumption of supersized amounts of fast food and soft drinks while doing it (*You have to use both hands*). Of course it can be argued that there are no publicly-funded physical conditioning or sporting facilities nearby (*How about getting off the couch and start by walking somewhere?*).

This health argument is being held in the public domain, but it is the same one inside the organization. We are way too politically correct. With more that 70 percent of the North American population now considered overweight—Body Mass Index (BMI) greater than 25—we may have already lost the democratic battle to reverse the trend in society, but it may not be too late to wage the war internally. In the organization, we called our reversal attempt wellness programs, in which unfortunately only 10–20 percent of colleagues participate—and they are generally those who need them the least. Hopefully, private sector organizations can do a much better job than governments and reverse the trend internally. According to a July 2006 article published in the Journal of Occupational & Environmental Medicine[30], for every one-point increase in an individual's BMI, the expected annual medical and drug costs increase by four percent and seven percent respectively.

I learned in the pharmaceutical industry the power of emotional marketing, where drug compliance and the call for action is often triggered by fear of dying. One of the best ways to achieve this is to invite colleagues to take part in a Health Risk Assessment (lifestyle, weight, blood work), and report to them their resulting accelerated aging. Healthcare insurance programs rarely reward people for exhibiting intelligent wellness behaviours. Drivers are awarded discounts on their auto insurance based on their driving record. Shouldn't colleagues who exercise, watch their weight, stop smoking, and adopt other healthy and preventative measures benefit as part of a workplace culture that rewards the right behaviours? The notion of consumerism is also very effective at providing a disincentive to consume healthcare—and consequently think prevention—when a co-pay fee is charged to users, and the totality of premiums are not reimbursed by the organization. We then take away the misperception that healthcare is free, simply because it is free to the beneficiary.

We have all heard of the fear management technique (*Michael Moore - Bowling for Columbine*) used by those who financially benefit from the sale of firearms, security, and warfare systems. It works admirably well into scaring people into taking action by supporting military expenditures, buying handguns and installing home-security systems. Fear management needs to be applied to healthcare. One may argue that we are smart enough to connect the dots and understand that these lifestyle choices are killing us, and that we don't need to be scared into doing something about it. Sadly, most human beings believe that they will defy the odds, and will not be the victim of the statistical probability *(Being statistically challenged is probably why they also buy lottery tickets)*. We all know one person who smoked like a chimney or was obese, and lived happily to be 97 years old *(That will be us)*.

A report published in 2005 by the World Health Organization (WHO) showed that if the chronic diseases controllable risk factors were eliminated, at least 80 percent of all heart disease, stroke and type-2 diabetes would be prevented, and over 40 percent of cancer would be prevented. The risk factors are: unhealthy diet and excessive energy intake, physical inactivity, and tobacco use. According to a 2009 report by the US Centers for Disease Control and Prevention, 75 percent of US health care spending is on people with chronic conditions and seven out of ten deaths among Americans each year are from chronic diseases.

Retirement

There has been a rapid evolution of retirement plans in the past 20-30 years from the legacy defined-benefit to defined-contribution plans. The number of pension plans today represents about 20-30 percent of what they used to be 25 years ago. What this means is that the Return-On-Investment (ROI) risk has been shifted from the employer to the colleague. The employer used to promise a comfortable retirement, regardless of how the financial markets performed. Now, the individual has to manage their retirement investment portfolio over the course of a working life to make sure they have the necessary financial means to allow for an adequate retirement *(The return-on-investment risk has now shifted from the organization to the colleagues)*.

According to the US Bureau of Labor Statistics, with the decline of defined-benefit/pension plans and major fluctuations in stock markets, the Baby Boomers, who are getting ready to retire, will increasingly need to rely on part-time work following their retirement to supplement their post-retirement income. They thought that their investments of the last decade would pay off, that their houses would be worth a lot more, and that their medical costs would be reasonable. Think again – the Standard & Poor's 500 index has posted total returns of just four percent since the beginning of the year 2000, the housing crash has erased about 35 percent of the value of their homes, and the average retiree will need close to $200,000 to fund post-retirement medical costs alone. Their parents, from the Swing generation (born 1928-45), don't have the same issue, as they will rely on their pension plan. In fact, if they worked for GM, they are one of 450,000 retirees who will draw from the $100 billion plan assets (*No wonder defined-benefit plans are out! The life expectancy of retirees also went up by 20 years from the 1930s, which means a huge incremental drain on the assets*).

The Swingers were probably not any more clever or better retirement planners than the next cohort to hit the working population, but their somewhat paternalistic employers were. The employers invested on their behalf to fund their future retirement. There is a case for organizations to be somewhat paternalistic when it comes to retirement, as most young colleagues, because of where they are in their life and career cycle (educational debt, young children) are not thinking about saving for their retirement (*Most of us as young adults never thought we would die, let alone ever retire*).

In this now-normal era of defined-contribution plans, investing early in a career is the best way to go, and let's face it; most of us would have not done it had we had a choice, which is why I believe in colleagues having to invest a minimum amount towards retirement. The infamous retirement-planning seminar, where the effect of compounded returns and cost-escalating effects of inflation are explained and discussed, needs to be attended by everyone, including the Millennials (*And they probably need to be scared into getting ready - fear works*).

Intangibles

The intangible aspects of total rewards are often underestimated and miscommunicated, probably because of their inherent nature and because they don't find their way on a pay stub or taxable-income statement. These intangibles are part of the brand, the deal or value proposition that can be quantified, but are not about the hard and tangible sticker price *(Remember, it is really about what the colleague gets when buying a career)*. They are the ancillary rewards of working here, and support core values. The relative value of these intangibles fluctuates depending on each individual, and where they are on their life and career cycles. The key intangibles that are part of the deal are those typically associated with the career-development and work/life balance aspects of the deal, which both can be quantified and costed out. These two aspects also happen to be part of key drivers of colleague engagement.

The career development intangibles are those that allow a colleague to either acquire new competencies, or enhance their proficiency in a particular area. The acquisition or enhancement of competencies is supportive of career progression and advancement, and, therefore, the creation of incremental wealth for the individual. These take the form of formal training, seminars, educational subsidies, developmental assignments, or career coaching—the organization is investing in my development.

Work/life balance intangibles are those rewards which allow and respect an individual's determination and management of the desired level of balance between their professional and personal life. That balance is not only individual, but it is also determined based on where the individual is in their life cycle. For instance, a young, single, ambitious colleague may have a different definition of work/life balance than a middle-aged single parent with two young children. The ability to take time off work—or the flexibility to buy more—or work from a location other than the place of work (telecommuting) in order to achieve the required balance is very valuable. Some of the best organizations (*I was wise enough to work for several*) will readily offer a reduced workweek to colleagues for parental, health, or lifestyle reasons. Don't let the business case fool you into believing that this is an expensive reward. This benefit allows organizations to have multiple colleagues available to perform the role, prevents retention risks from materializing, and enhances colleague engagement. The on-site provision of time-consuming personal-life activities (Figure 67) has also become very popular, particularly since the emergence of the dual-income family unit. In short, the ability to choose the appropriate work/life balance is a key factor in engaging and attracting talent.

- Medical Clinic
- Fitness Training
- Banking
- Dry Cleaning
- Vehicle Service Pick-up
- Take-home Meals
- Food Service
- Childcare
- Concierge Service

FIGURE 67 — TIMESAVING ONSITE SERVICES

TALENT PLANNING—HAVING THE RIGHT TALENT IN THE RIGHT ROLE TODAY AND FOR TOMORROW

It is now clear to most private and public sector organizations (*Took long enough, didn't it?*) that the only way to be successful at achieving anything is to have the right people in the organization, and enough of them, at any point in time when they are needed. There is always the option of replacing the people we have with the ones we need when necessary, or to outsource the work to someone who has them. In the end, the only difference is who owns the employment relationship, because someone has to think about either getting people ready, or finding those who are.

Talent planning is the organization's part of the two-part game of matching defined roles to interested and competent individuals. The other part is career development, which is the responsibility of the individual. The talent plan assumes that individuals want to develop and progress, and build career and wealth, therefore not wanting to stagnate in the same role for a lifetime. They will either migrate internally, or leave the organization. It also assumes that the organization's industry, strategy, and business plan will change dramatically over time, which in turn will mean changing structure and roles and ultimately the competencies required to fulfil the roles.

The strategic aspect of talent planning is about attempting to forecast and manage the impact of the business strategy, demographics, and employment market trends on the organization's ability to attract the required number of right people and ensure that current colleagues develop the right competencies at the right pace. While the discussions take place at the enterprise level—typically during the annual strategic-thinking process—the execution of the plan happens at the micro-level, between each team leader and team member as well as in between each team leader and their HR business partner and/or talent-acquisition SME. In certain specific cases—such as the implementation of an ERP—most roles in the organization would be impacted; in such cases a massive competency-development exercise would have to be undertaken at the enterprise level. The entry of the organization in a new product or technology sector would have a similar impact.

The risk-management aspect of the same process used to be called succession planning, where we would sit down and assess the potential retention and/or retirement risks for the incumbents of critical roles only, as it would have been impossible to carry it out for the entire organization. At the global level, we would typically review the two organizational levels below the Chief Executive. The Board would look after potential successors to the Chief Executive. We would identify internal and external candidates who could either hold the fort for a while or could be promoted into a role left vacant by a departing colleague having resigned, retired, or whose employment would have been terminated.

The annointment of the successor was not that great of a process, as it would automatically send a damaging career and motivational signal to the other candidates, who may or may not have had the patience to stick around for the next round of succession planning and hopefully get the prize. In those days, not much conversation would occur with potential successors regarding their career ambitions and plans, as the assumption was that everyone wanted to be promoted. The irony of it was that the risk management plan was actually creating incremental retention risks. Too many times, the annointed one, in whom a disproportionate level of development resources had been invested, would either be lured away or promoted by a competitor before the succession plan could be implemented, or would no longer be the choice of a newly-appointed leader (*Some of the successors actually were the object of employment termination by the same newly-appointed leader – go figure*).

After having figured out that our attempt to unilaterally crystal ball the future at that granular level, without great input from colleagues themselves, we evolved. We figured out that the likelihood of being successful at globally managing the domino effect within a nine-layer organization every time a successor needed to, and was willing to, be assigned was insane. Legacy succession planning is an irresponsible fallacy.

The better way to manage the risk is now known as talent planning, where the objective is to invest in the development of every colleague in order to develop a pool, or bench strength, of interested and competent candidates to choose from either as successors or to be assigned to new roles created as a result of growth (*Succession planning does not work very well in a shrinking organization, needless to say*). There is not much sense in developing an individual for a future role they have no career interest in.

The real value of a development program, either for single-contributor talent or leadership talent, lies in the predictability of the outcome and its alignment to business objectives (*Yes, you can waste a lot of development dollars in the ad-hoc way, but that cost is peanuts in comparison to the business impact of not achieving the talent-development strategy*). The absence of a plan tends to promote the assignment of individuals to development events or courses only because of the successful marketing contained in the brochure that reached your inbox.

In the past, the succession planning process would entail getting incumbents from the same level in the organization to review data related to each colleague from the two levels below their own. They would review, as a group, individual data output from the performance development process, organizational surveys, 360-degree feedback surveys, and career development. The process would generate great discussions about each individual and potential future role, but would also serve as a calibration event. It would become very evident in the room when one of the reviewers was out of step with their colleagues in terms of their assessment of a particular team member when the individual would be deemed to be 'walking on water' by their team leader while being assessed as a 'sinker' by everyone else there. The greatest of debates, if not arguments—would focus on an individual's alignment and respect of the organization's core values *(It is fascinating to see how quickly a team leader's clashing values get brought up in 360-degree surveys, or how rapidly these values get promulgated vertically by their disciples).*

The norm in the talent planning/succession world is to attempt to plot every individual in the talent pool on the infamous nine-box grid (Figure 68), where performance and potential are the two axes used to drop each individual into one of the boxes. There are several versions of the terminology to define what each box means, and what development action should be taken *(I just picked one version here as an example).*

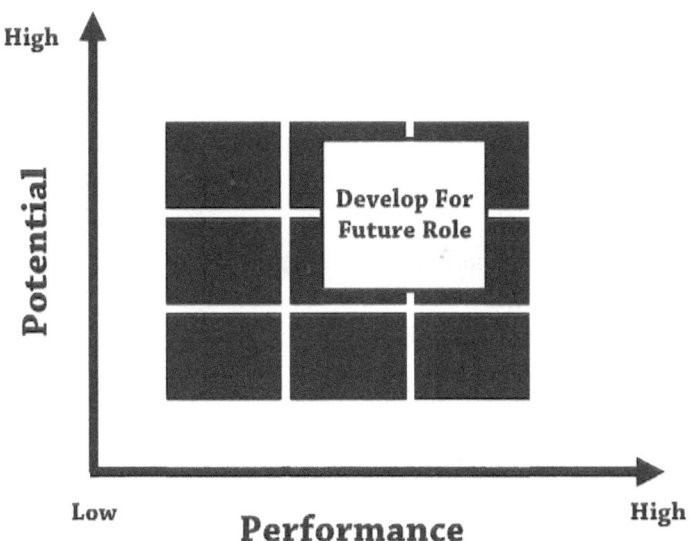

FIGURE 68 — NINE-BOX TALENT REVIEW GRID

The tool is said *(I am not sure it is true, but whatever...)* to have had its genesis in the 1970s, when the Boston Consulting Group (BCG) developed the 'Boston Matrix' which uses market growth and market share as a way of screening market opportunities and determines which market to invest in. General Electric asked consulting firm, McKinsey & Company, to create a similar model that better suited its needs. The result was the 3x3 GE-McKinsey Matrix, also called the Nine-Box Matrix/Grid.

It is uncertain as to how the GE matrix evolved into the performance/potential grid though it is reasonable to assume that it was adapted to determine which individuals to invest in. Hypothetically, those colleagues deemed to be high performers and high potentials should be the object of more significant talent development and total rewards investments than others. Again, that elitist approach has the risk of creating two distinct classes of citizens—the stars, and the rest of us.

The more modern outlook on developmental investment should be based on the assumption that such high-potential talent will learn and develop quickly and therefore will require significant investment to satisfy this insatiable hunger for incremental competencies and accountabilities. Development investment should come as needed and should provide an adequate performance return on development invested. There is a danger in assigning a disproportionate amount of development resources to the chosen few only. The disengagement impact on the rest of the population far outweighs the engagement enhancement of such a small segment. Of course, we want to believe that we will keep it secret and that no one will find out, but they always do.

The tool is very popular, but has its inherent risks and flaws. The tool assumes that the inputs for the plotting of performance ratings and potential are indeed reliable. Only three levels of performance ratings are available, which breaks the rule of 'don't allow a middle of the road rating'.

Also the ratings carry the assumption that a high-output colleague, regardless of their alignment to the behaviours associated with core values, is deemed a high performer. The other risk is the arbitrary assignment of potential level.

> *Potential:* Something that can develop or become actual. An ability that someone has that can be developed to help that person become successful

The question of potential is asked for planning purposes. The organization is asking itself if further developmental investment is warranted to support the performance and career development of a colleague. When an individual has achieved their full potential, it means that there is minimal room or capacity left to accept incremental accountabilities and effectively acquire the competencies associated with them, which is why a competency model is critical. If the challenge of a role is being defined as the depth, breadth, and amount of information to be integrated when making decisions, not to mention the time horizon over which the impact of those decisions have to be made, then potential means how much of each an incumbent is ultimately capable of handling.

The erroneous assumption, when doing talent planning, is that the organization is developing future team leaders. The real question should be, 'Bob or Suzie has potential to do what'? rather then having potential or not. Potential may be to handle more technical/functional accountabilities rather than progression to the next leadership level.

The need to assign incumbents with adequate potential to any role is simply a means of mitigating the risk of a role getting away from them. An incumbent suddenly feeling overwhelmed or 'in over their head' is normally a symptom of either potential not having been developed to the right level, or the role becoming heavier than expected. In this era of consolidation, diversification, and globalization (*We have already gone through the era of delayering, flattening and right sizing*), the demands normally placed on any particular role, often suddenly become more stringent.

A similar phenomenon occurs when young, high-growth organizations suddenly find that the incumbents they had originally brought in start to struggle with increasing velocity and mass. I call it the volcano effect. The individuals and leaders get promoted by the organization's sheer growth, rather than by thoughtful design and careful upgrading of its talent. The outcome is often a massive organizational eruption, leading to failure or massive loss of shareholder value. It is true that the fluid and chaotic environments of start-ups often does not suit the process-driven and systematic framework of larger entities, but it tends to be the exponential complexity of its roles which strains potential. The demands of playing high-school football versus NCAA are a quantum leap higher. The demands of today's global organization have shifted from being simply complicated to highly complex.

The intricacy of potential is that it is very difficult to assess early in a career, and that it needs to be developed over time. The capability of an individual can be observed at any point and time (Figure 69), and the speed at which the capacity was reached can also be measured. That developmental speed is probably one of the most simple and reliable predictors of full or end-game potential.

It is difficult not to equate potential with intellect, as development occurs through learning, and the performance of complex roles also requires superior intellect. However, other interpersonal and leadership competencies—related to EQ—are also often required to perform such demanding roles. It is easier to predict that an individual has the potential to handle a role one hierarchic level (i.e. L1, L2, L3) higher in the next 3 years, than to have predicted, 30 years ago, that Bill Gates and Microsoft were going to impact the planet over the course of several generations. However, an individual who repeatedly performs at superior levels when promoted is likely to be considered a high potential. The speed of development is naturally related to the quantity, quality, and diversity of the developmental investments and resources. Young hockey players who already dominate their league at a young age and continue to do so at each level are identified as having NHL potential and are assigned to elite teams, where they receive more and better developmental coaching.

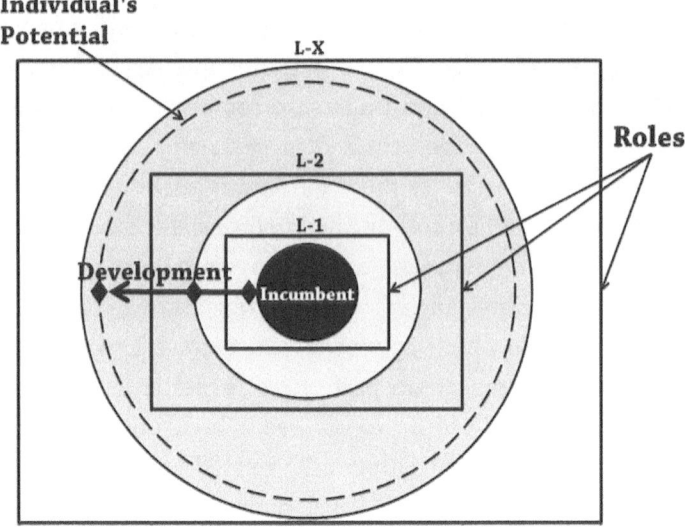

FIGURE 69 — INDIVIDUAL AND ROLE POTENTIAL LEVELS

CAREER DEVELOPMENT—PEOPLE GETTING THEMSELVES READY

The common colleague, (*Like most of us without a divinity syndrome*), who needs to work and earn a living, aspires to reach a point where they can look back and state unequivocally that they have a nice career behind them. We are not in control of our career going forward, but rather we aim at developing it and should have a plan to get there. Unfortunately, the plan may or may not be successfully implemented. Most of us, when we entered the workforce, wanted to have a nice career, make more money, and maybe even impact or change the world. Some of us went to university and invested a substantial amount of money to get a head start at getting that career (*Probably the best investment you can make in return for a lifetime annuity of compensation*). But we did not really have a plan—we had ambition and dreams and figured that, if we worked hard for the right organization, we would enhance our chances of making it.

For many years, we expected increasingly over-burdened and sub-competent team leaders to be great career advisers to their team members. Unfortunately, too few of them were prepared to unselfishly coach one of their own team members, particularly if they considered a star would seek developmental career assignments outside of their own teams. Many organizations assigned these mentors, who were respected colleagues with no line of authority, to their pupils (*In the end, they were all well-intended amateurs*). We now assign certified and independent career coaches to developing colleagues. Many organizations, unfortunately, reserve the provision of such services to high potentials only, in whom they believe investment is warranted (*Another example of an intangible benefit which screams of class-citizenship, and backfires as a bad cultural message*).

The career coach is probably, (*My logical guess*), an evolved version of the high-school career or guidance counsellor, a role that became necessary in the post-industrial late 20th century when suddenly a multitude of career choices were becoming available. The numerous down cycles of the global economy exposed workers to these career coaches who were part of the career-transition or outplacement services offered to individuals whose employment relationship had be severed, either as part of a mass layoff or Reduction In Force (RIF)—or simply because they had been fired. The career coach's mission is to help the individual identify and secure alternative employment or get refurbished into another occupation or industry where demand for talent exists. For the most difficult cases, where a person's employment has been terminated for behavioural or cultural-misfit reasons, the coach embarks on a remedial process to find corrective solutions to the counter-productive behaviours.

As the newer generations of colleagues came on line, we started to see a much more decisive and demanding approach to career development. The combination of impatience, ambition, and superficial knowledge of the career and talent-development world has the requisite elements for a perfect turnover storm. Colleagues are not prepared to wait for the organization —or allow it for that matter— to make career decisions on their behalf. With the upcoming shortage of talent, these free agents are likely to move around quite a bit. Internal career opportunities and development are key factors in candidates joining and remaining with an organization.

The leading-edge organizations are already taking action to prevent the storm from happening in their own microclimate backyard. They are better equipping their team leaders, and are offering career development support by providing formal career-development resources, and third-party coaches.

In the past, organizations had developed these career paths that more or less predetermined the sequential steps an individual would have to take in order to climb the organizational ladder. These paths tragically assumed that the only way for an individual to progress financially was to become a manager. After decades of failed managers, leading-edge technology organizations finally figured out that to promote the best scientist or engineer into a managerial role—let alone a leadership one—was to lose a great technical contributor only to gain a sub-optimal manager. The same phenomenon was occurring with high-performance sales individuals. The dual career path was invented to allow these technical single contributors to progress financially and career wise without having to join the management ranks. The real question then should be again: a colleague has the potential to become what?

The old-style career paths were rigid and did not really support lateral movement across functions and families of roles, nor did they support the notion of transferability of competencies across functions. People were confined to move within their own specific functional silo in an upward domino sequence. In reality, the only true career paths were those observed in retrospect. Modern career-paths are very fluid and customized—the legacy career ladder is often referred to as a career lattice to reflect the fact that career progression now often takes a lateral path rather than only an upward or vertical one.

The key to injecting fluidity in the career-management process rested with the total rewards SMEs figuring out how to recognize the value of technical contribution and the distilling of roles into competencies. The modern systems now provide feedback to colleagues on their competency progression through the performance-development program, and provide full visibility on the competency requirements of any and every role within the organization. Colleagues then clearly see what development is needed for them to match the competency requirements of any role they wish to postulate for. The families of roles, or functions, still exist (e.g. sales, manufacturing, and finance) but they now outline the natural progression of roles when either enhanced proficiency or incremental competencies are achieved in a continuum.

It was difficult enough before for a colleague to manage one career. Now comes an emerging trend where individuals invest in multiple careers, either sequentially or in parallel. In her 2007 book entitled *One Person/Multiple Career*[31], Marci Alboher uses the term 'slashers' to describe colleagues who express their parallel occupations, using several descriptors separated by slashes (*This, somehow, has way more cachet than moonlighting*). Famous U2 vocalist Bono, for example, is now considered to be a rock-star/humanitarian (*The earliest of that phenomenon was probably the 'dashing' working-mother, wasn't it?*).

The demographic profile of the current workforce makes it far more proficient than their predecessors at finding out which industry and organizations can offer them the career and environment they are looking for. Their career choices, however, are not so much driven by the likelihood of securing gainful employment post-graduation, but rather their personal interest and passions. Too many governments and academic institutions, and in particular universities, continue to resist partnering with industry to forecast its future employment needs and produce employment-market ready talent. More than ever, the organization's ability to recognize the transferability of the knowledge and competencies they would have acquired in unrelated roles will be key in retaining, developing, and attracting talent.

There are a growing number of university students who drop out to enlist in the vastly cheaper junior or community colleges to increase the return on their educational investment, by rapidly getting a money-making/salary-paying occupation. According to the Conference Board, "Recent research suggests that the field of study may be more important than the type of academic institution attended. Perhaps the distinction between college and university is less important than the relevance of the discipline to the workplace, since it is relevance—along with supply and demand—that sets the market price for skilled talent".

My advice and firm belief of career management *(And I happen to have pro-actively and successfully managed my own over the years)* is that life and career are too short to suffer the pain and agony of disengagement, frustration, and unhappiness associated with being with someone with whom you don't want to work with doing something you are not passionate about *(A great leader I worked for early in my career used to say, "Life is not a dress rehearsal; this is the real thing!")*. You will never be great at something you are not passionate about. Great lives and great careers occur when growth, either professional or personal, is the driving force. Growth creates opportunities to learn, develop, and achieve. Any relationship, be it employment or personal, can no longer be honestly committed to for a lifetime. Rather, both parties have to commit to invest in the relationship, and revisit their engagement every three to five years *(No, I am not a marriage counsellor, but I tend to follow my own advice)*. It is unrealistic to expect either party to continue if the other party is not living up to their part of the bargain. Organizations and partners will change, and we should all reserve the right not to continue if the change is dramatically unfavourable to either our career or life plan.

EMPLOYMENT SEVERANCE—PARTING WITH THOSE NO LONGER NEEDED OR WANTED

The end of a career or tenure, regardless of the motive, is an emotionally traumatic event for all of the parties involved, particularly to the departing colleague (*And if it is not, the severance is probably warranted and long overdue!*). The departing individual is either going to become an alumni and future ambassador, or will make it their mission to let the world know about how awful it was to work there and how badly they were treated on their way out. The remaining colleagues will interpret the way they were treated, good or bad, as the way they themselves will be treated when, and if, their time comes. If there is one process that must past the organization's core values test, it is the employment termination one. How a colleague's employment relationship is terminated is quite the cultural statement.

I have been torn for years, (*Maybe the word is too strong, ambivalent is better*) about the best way to proceed. I have argued with colleagues, who have disagreed with our best-in-class employment severance process, which had been vetted by leading-edge consultants. Giving no advanced notice to a colleague, asking them to leave the premises immediately, while escorted by a career transition counsellor, and removing all physical and technological access was deemed to be the right thing to do. The logic behind the process is to mitigate the vindictive and confidentiality risk to the organization, to protect the dignity of the individual, and to minimize the emotional impact of a potentially distraught individual on by-standing colleagues. Needless to say, my legal counsel colleagues would generally support the risk-free and reasonably heartless approach, attempting to fend off potential lawsuits. Some of my CFO colleagues would support the equally heartless, cost-effective no-severance approach (*Here is a perfect example of the value of diversity of thought and debate in a leadership team... and why neither finance nor legal counsel should be allowed to decide on the severance approach*).

The counter argument to that process, and the criticism from the more compassionate or sensitive colleagues, is that such an approach does not align with the organization's core values. Asking a colleague to depart immediately, often with a security escort, and removing access to work premises and information systems could be perceived as disrespectful and distrusting of a previously valued and respected colleague. This is where the circumstances of the severance and the individual's character must be taken into consideration; flexibility and judgement in the approach is key. What is undoubtedly unfair to a colleague is not having provided them with feedback, and therefore affording them no opportunity to correct the counterproductive behaviours or performance deficiencies which ultimately led to the severance in the first place. The individual's team leader must be held accountable for allowing such tragic occurrences.

The employment-termination process, like most other processes, often suffers from a lack of transparency and understanding. Every colleague deserves to know and understand what will happen to them should their employment be terminated, rather than infer and speculate based on their observations of how colleagues have been treated in the past. In short, the employment termination policy needs to be published, complete with severance amount calculations. Having only senior executives know their severance conditions through their employment contract is another ill-advised and legacy hierarchic phenomenon.

Offering career transition support is a great practice, which not only helps a departed colleague to better deal with the severance trauma, reflect on their career and performance, and secure the right alternative employment quicker, but also enables the organization to keep track of how the former colleague is doing in the search process. People want to know how a departed colleague is doing. However, with the wireless and internet technology available now, providing expensive real estate space to an individual to carry out job searching from is no longer necessary. Face-to-face coaching remains very important though.

INTERNAL COMMUNICATIONS MANAGEMENT—HOLDING THE ENTERPRISE DIALOGUE

The ability for an organization, its teams and people to effectively communicate, either good news or bad news (*Not telling bad news is not telling the whole truth*) is probably the most critical element in fostering an environment of trust. Trust will not occur without truth. Truth, facts, issues, and opportunities can be acted upon almost in an instantaneous fashion, without unnecessary deliberation, consuming the decoding, second-guessing, and vetting energy required dealing with doubt and opacity.

Many people wrongfully believe that dealing with 'the brutal facts' (*Collins in Good to Great*[15]) is difficult. They think this can cause conflict and damage relationships, and that communicating bad news will undermine people's engagement. Bad news tends to travel fast in the form of rumours which take on a magnitude of their own as a snow ball does, and does not provide people with the opportunity to deal with and manage the real and factual bad news. This is not only inappropriate, but also disrespectful to colleagues. The term 'brutal facts' does not imply to be disrespectful, violent or impolite in the delivery of the facts, but rather to deliver the raw, unedited and naked truth without the so-called 'political' frosting. The vintage practice of giving the news the right 'spin', arrogantly assumes that the targeted recipients are hostage to only one source of information, or intellectually limited enough to buy the spin. (*If that is the case, the larger problem is to knowingly accept the fact that this is the sorry state of our colleague population...so much for high-performance dreams*). What kills colleague engagement (*And also stock markets*) is the paralyzing effect of uncertainty and speculation.

Effective communication, by definition, involves a two-way process with minimal filtering or interference, with a feedback loop to validate its correct interpretation. It is hard enough to achieve effective communication between two individuals, which gets compounded by the size and diversity of the audience, either at the team or organizational level. In a global context, language and cultural filters add even further challenges to the process. Organizational or corporate communications, often referred to as corporate talk, are often perceived as such and lose the airwave battle by giving way to alternative channels or rumours, perceived to be carrying accurate and timely information. Do you really believe that the Russian population believed and relied upon *Pravda* for the truth? We all want highly engaged colleagues, but that level of engagement demands that colleagues be constantly and consistently communicated with and not simply communicated at.

The current colleague population, and particularly the Gen-Xers and Millennials, has mastered the art of instantaneous and mass-distributed information. With all of the blogs and social networking capabilities, whoever believes that information, can be hidden from the organization for more than a few minutes should have been a *Jurassic Park* cast member. As Elvis Presley once said, "Truth is like the sun. You can shut it out for a time, but it ain't goin' away." We used to struggle to manage the conflict between internal and external communications when the stories to shareholders did not match those published internally, but censorship is now a futile exercise. Any mass communication to colleagues inevitably triggers conversations amongst team members and questions to their team leader. It is incongruous to expect that team leaders will be effective primary information sources without treating them accordingly by providing them with advanced and enhanced communication material. There is nothing worse for a team leader to say than, "I don't know any more than you do", or "They, don't tell us anything."

Highly engaged team members not only expect to be communicated with, but also expect to be consulted. They can deal with decisions being made even if not in total agreement, so long as they clearly understand the logic, and had an opportunity to voice their opinions or concerns before the decision was made. What colleagues despise are decisions impacting them having been made without having involved them or a trusted representative. They consider that to be disrespectful and unconducive to teamwork. In a non-unionized environment, we would create a consultation structure for that purpose.

ALUMNI MANAGEMENT—KEEPING IN TOUCH WITH FORMER COLLEAGUES

The universities are probably the most experienced at managing their relationship with alumni, with the professional services or consulting firms being a close second. Universities keep in touch with their former students, counting on their emotional connection and gratitude, to entice them into supporting the school's fund-raising campaigns. The showcasing of famous successful alumni also helps with student recruiting. Former students also want to stay connected with fellow students out of friendship, simple curiosity, or for business-development purposes.

The consulting firms who pioneered the corporate alumni networks hoped that a departing alumna would go on to become a leader in an organization, and would subsequently do business with their alma mater, or even rejoin the firm someday. Some alumni programs are initiated though a grass-roots movement in order to simply keep in touch and maintain valued personal relationships with colleagues. Many of those are simply ad-hoc groups of colleagues who would have had close relationships (*The risk of any relationship-based selling or buying, alumni related or not, is that one of the parties is likely to pay too much, or not get the best product or service as a trade-off for that relationship. Wal-Mart is famous for not allowing its buyers to have any personal relationship with its suppliers*).

Many large organizations would have retiree associations, where the membership criteria would be to have officially retired from the organization after a certain number of years, or be receiving a retirement annuity. The members typically get the organization's newsletter, purchasing discounts, and are invited to the annual retirement party or company picnic. Those having left the organization before retirement are typically not invited (*This practice is not that clever in this short-tenure day and age. It is always better to err on the side of inclusivity*).

The explosion of social networking, and in particular LinkedIn™, the war for talent, the cyclical hiring and de-hiring blitz, and the shortening of tenure driven by generational profiles are now making the investment in alumni management an evidently smart one. The networking provides access to pre-vetted candidates—alumni tend to recommend candidates who fit well into the organization—and allows for the re-recruiting or boomerang recruiting of former colleagues. The exception to that rule is those awful organizations that turn over their staff at a frightening rate, and generate gigantic alumni. The secret to any successful alumni association is that the answer to the alumni's 'what's in it for me' question be such that they would want to join and actively participate, and that doing so is easy and simple because of technology enablement. It has to be an easy two-way street.

COMPLIANCE MANAGEMENT—STAYING AWAY FROM FINES AND JAIL

The legal jurisdictions of the world, from municipal to federal, and even global, have all come up with legislation regarding how to deal with human beings in an organizational context. Most legislation came out as a result of some special-interest group exercising political pressure on democratically elected governments to protect human beings from some aspect of organizational life, probably in return for a promise to support their election (*I am not sure dictators and despots really care about the topic – do you think?*). Somewhere in history, that protection was necessary and the intent of the legislation was sound and honourable. Labor unions deserve the credit for having been at the forefront of influencing the debate (*Which is a sad statement on the quality of the leadership of the organizations which was neither enlightened nor magnanimous enough to figure out what the right thing to do was until it was legislated into doing it. So much for leadership!*).

Sadly, labour unions were created out of a real and perceived need to protect workers from their companies and their leaders (*And I am using the term loosely*). These organizations truly deserved the unions they ended up with. That need, however, appears to be diminishing according to the US Bureau of Labor Statistics. In 2010, the union membership rate, the percent of wage-and-salary workers who were members of a union, stood at 11.9 percent, down from 12.3 percent a year earlier. In 1983, the union membership rate was 20.1 percent.

The real cost of organized labour is not in higher wages and lower productivity, but rather in its inherent rigidity and lack of responsiveness to today's competitive, change and adaptive imperatives. It is worth pointing out that most non-represented organizations actually provide higher total compensation packages than their union counterparts as a means of preventing unionization, thus buying full change flexibility. They ironically also create an open-door colleague-consultation structure, which looks an awful lot like what a labour union would install.

The anti-legislation pundits will argue that the legislation negatively impacts competitiveness by adding unnecessary costs and delays to the process of conducting business, particularly when it comes to competing with developing jurisdictions that don't have to comply with such legislation. I somehow cannot believe that having access to all of those capital, technological, and human resources is not enough to level the playing field between our legislated industrial world and the fledgling free-wheeling Third World (*Give me a break*).

Most of us know by now that the intent of the legislation was sound and that the intent was right. We don't really need legislation to make us do it any more than we need the threat of an expensive ticket to wear a seatbelt. The fallacy around what we call labour legislation is that it is way too easy to hide behind the legislation and collective agreements, rather than simply do the right thing. American scholar and pioneer of the contemporary field of leadership studies, Warren Bennis, said, "Leaders are people who do the right thing; managers are people who do things right."

What unfortunately took us away from the intent and meaning of the legislation was the pervasive and obsessive need of the legal profession to argue the text of the law, rather than its original intent. Legislation is about social values, as religion once was. It is developed and written by mortal humans—not gods.

Too many organizations and their Human Resources apostles try to justify and sell the need to lead the right way by threatening the consequences of breaking the law, rather than simply showing the intrinsic value of doing it the right way. Not engaging in discrimination, sexual harassment, or unsafe and inequitable work practices is not about obeying the law. It is about believing and ethically recognizing that there is a moral, factual, and business reason for doing so. Organizations want to access the totality of the talent pool, promote the best, behave appropriately so as to support colleague engagement, and protect individuals against harm (*And if they don't, they should*).

While I am a self-confessed and known critic of organized religion—and organized labour for that matter—most of the fundamental edicts and values are sound. If there was one principle anyone should adhere to, it is the age-old Golden Rule adhered to by all religions, which states, "One should treat others as one would like others to treat oneself".

PERFORMANCE EQUATION

The dream of every organization (*If not it should be...*) is to achieve the best effectiveness and efficiency possible, and to sustain it. Just simply being better than the competitor is a risky proposition, as it may well be that the competitor is awful, and we are just less awful than they are. We have all used different expressions to describe what being 'great at it' means. How about a few of these expressions: World-class, Major league, Formula 1, Top 100.

The one thing that each of those expressions has in common, is that it intrinsically refers to a group of peers, a class or a league in which competition occurs. The only way to know how great we are is to compare ourselves against others in the top league, and keep score, which is why I am a big fan of benchmarking and metrics. The one risk of benchmarking though is to fail to recognize that the top players are already on their way to improving their game as well. So the best approach is not to aim for where they are, but rather for where they are going (*Wayne Gretzky once said, "A good hockey player plays where the puck is. A great hockey player plays where the puck is going to be."*).

In striving to become great, there is nothing easier than to understand and copy those who already are and work with the partners they signed up to help them get and stay there. There is no wisdom in attempting to re-invent the wheel. To pretend that all of the top players in the league are wrong and that our contradicting approach is right could well be a blatant case of irresponsible arrogance. Humility, or self-integrity, will prevent us from doing that but will also make it uncomfortable for us to call ourselves the best or the greatest even if we are absolutely sure that we are. It always feels better to be acknowledged by a respected third party than to boast and brag.

This is why I would rather refer to what I am about to describe as optimal vs. best or top operational effectiveness. This model, or equation, is about using fundamental, simple, and integrated people approaches and ideas, which are used by the top players in the league. Implementing them will not only get you in the league, but also will likely buy you a playoff spot, and maybe even the championship.

THE ROLE OF THE HR TEAM

There are no doubts remaining now—enough studies conducted, and books written—that demonstrate that the Human Resources team is trusted with the accountability to recommend the strategies, policies, programs, and processes necessary to support highly-engaged colleagues in driving a high-performance optimally-effective organization. More than ever now, the limited availability and volatility of talent, and the challenges of global competitiveness makes it of paramount importance that individuals and teams perform to their best (*I could have said Human Capital instead of talent, but the wording is reserved for the big accounting firms who dabble at the people game and try to resonate with their CFO audit clients and the financial sector*). The function was, is, and will continue to be a strategic one, which business leaders must insist is present at the leadership team table (*The old corporate services functions, inevitably led by the top-ranking accountant and encompassing finance, business technology, legal and HR should be extinct by now*). Being an amateur at any of those functions is not any more productive than to be an amateur at the finance and accounting level (*Here...I got it out of my system*).

The old personnel administration or labour relations types are no longer what is needed and should have been put out to pasture by now. The new generation of HR practitioners are top-notch business people who are customer focused, data driven, technology savvy, and who have solid consulting and project/process management competencies.

They are neither the advocates nor the adversaries of the company or the people. They are the advocates of high performance and productive relationships between those who seek rewarding careers, and those who seek innovation and performance. Their role is one of trusted and impartial business and career advisers. They are not to be the surrogates for those team leaders whose abdication inevitably leads to sub-optimal performance and engagement. The primary bond and relationship, and accountability for engagement and performance, must be between a team member, their colleagues, and the team leader—not the HR business partner.

HR practitioners are also accountable to audit and enforce people policies, programs and processes as well as culture. The police component of their role requires not only diligence, but courage and support from the organization to do so—further reasons why HR people and the CHRO need clearly-defined authorities and severance benefits as a deterrent to those tempted to apply pressure on them to look the other way, or simply keep quiet.

Leading-edge human resources teams understand business and strive to operate like commercial service-delivery organizations. They emulate the best of service providers and consulting firms in how they cost-effectively develop, market, sell, and support their products and services. They understand that the HR team is not only there as a catalyst, but also a role model (*How can you be passionate about this stuff, and not live it every day and be the best at it?*). They engender career customer loyalty by exceeding expectations and offering consistent and recurring delightful experiences.

They model themselves, learn from, and admire the best innovators and customer-focused organizations and brands in the world and know from experience that it's all about people. Not surprisingly, the Bloomberg Business Week's list of best client-pleasing brands is determined by rating both the organization's people and its processes and by asking how many clients would definitely recommend the brand. The Four Seasons Hotel chain consistently makes the top-five list and is often considered the worldwide role model.

Human resources practitioners will partner with leading HR and talent consulting firms to identify trends and best practices which can be effectively implemented, and how they can best organize themselves to deliver innovation and great internal customer service. The shared-services delivery model (Figure 70) is still the best, which happens to be how the best providers of commercial services, such as banks, telecoms, and airlines do it (*Beware of outsourcing career customers touch points—it has often backfired*). The size of the team does not matter, but the quality of the advice to team leaders, and level of service to colleagues does (*Using *a space shuttle to get around when an ultra-light will do could be over-kill*). Beware of those who want to apply too much HR technology. Yes, while it's true that those systems come with best practices and automated work flows, they can be overwhelming and require armies of people just to maintain them. Technology does not fix indigenous process or people problems; it makes them faster and bigger, and migrates issues from the real world to cyberspace. The zeroes and ones become the source of digital anxiety.

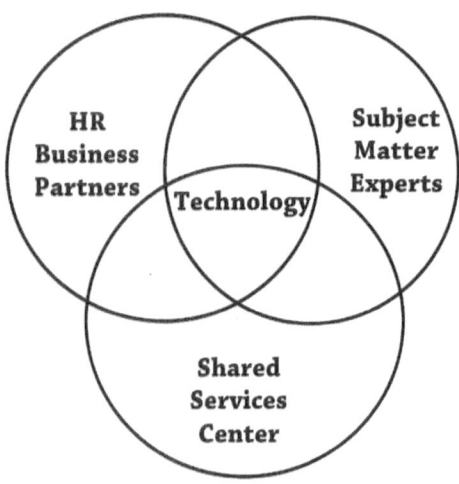

FIGURE 70 — SHARED SERVICES-DELIVERY MODEL ELEMENTS

It has always fascinated me that the leading human resources practices came from Silicon Valley and its supporting consulting firms there. It is not surprising since nowhere was the war for talent more heated, particularly in the dot-com boom of the '80s. The competitive advantage came directly from people with knowledge who were being innovative together as teams. The consulting firms from

California, and certainly the HR ones, also understood that not only was that phenomenon impacting them, but that if a colleague left the firm, often the clients followed. They realized that who they employed and what they sold were one in the same. Colleague turnover became not only costly in terms of performance and output, but in terms of client revenues and relationships. Product innovators and consulting firms had to be good at the 'HR thing', or they would have not made it.

THE EQUATION'S VARIABLES

When all is said, read, and done, the wisdom of authors, research of academics, and dogma of major-league players boils down to a pretty simple performance equation (*I had to fit that one in to match the title of the book*). The common denominators of the best models, expertise, and organizational know-how emerge as the fundamental variables (Figure 71) of a high-performance people organization.

1. The Mission, Vision & Strategy are clear and understood by all
2. The success culture is clearly stated and passionately defended
3. Well-engineered organization (structure, roles, processes)
4. Incumbents with great potential who 'fit' their role
5. Great 'personal' and 'Level-5' team leaders
6. Emotionally-engaged team members
7. Vertically and horizontally-aligned strategy-execution performance goals
8. Key Performance Indicators (KPIs), scorecard & benchmarks
9. People and teams are rewarded and recognized for disciplined execution
10. Open two-way communication & consultation

FIGURE 71 — PERFORMANCE EQUATION VARIABLES

THE MISSION, VISION, & STRATEGY ARE CLEAR AND UNDERSTOOD BY ALL

It kind of goes without saying that it's improbable that any organization would be able to perform well without understanding which game it's playing, their vision for the team, and the strategy they will use to win. But having a mission, vision, and strategy without communicating them to the team is not predictive of winning many games either. A former colleague of mine and a brilliant organizational development and metrics guru cautioned that, when measuring colleague awareness, survey results would often be misleadingly high as respondents would answer 'yes' to the question, 'I understand the organization's mission, vision and strategy.' He would grin, and say, "You'd get different results if you then ask: OK, so what is it?"

It is very difficult for individuals to pull their weight and line up their efforts without knowing what they are here for, where they dream of getting, and how they are going to get there. The analogy here would be a team of football players running onto the field without a game plan and with no huddle. It is also very difficult for them to explain or defend the organization if they are not aware of, or don't trust its plan. The trust and faith in the vision and strategy comes with the execution, tangible actions, and achievements of the plan, not the packaging. Corporate talk with no action, or the perception of no action breeds cynicism *(Q: What do you call someone whose words you perceive don't match their actions? A: A liar!)*.

THE SUCCESS CULTURE IS CLEARLY STATED AND PASSIONATELY DEFENDED

The aggregate core values of the organization, which we call culture, dictate how we will conduct business in order to be successful. The behaviours associated with each of its elements need to be passionately defended, and enforced. The organization's core values are embedded in all business processes—especially the people ones. In light of this, individuals achieving their objectives, while disrespecting any element of the culture, must be deemed to be non-performers.

The leader of each team, starting with the organization's Chief Executive, is accountable for role modelling and enforcing the culture and its behaviours. No colleague must ever be subjected to or held hostage to, inappropriate or counter-cultural behaviour while employed by the organization. While in a level of seriousness of its own, sexual harassment in the workplace is an identical phenomenon, and we rightfully deal harshly with those who are guilty of it. The disengagement of colleagues, or their departure from the organization is most often attributable to a conflict between their personal values and the behaviours of a team leader or their team. People don't often leave organizations. They leave their team leader.

Who could argue that the rate of change is constantly increasing and that those organizations and individuals who either resist the change or are unable to adapt to it will ultimately fail? We have used in vain the age-old expression 'Some people resist change', without really asking ourselves why. People don't resist change per se, they resist the perceived personal risk associated with it. More than ever, a culture where change and innovation are anticipated, encouraged, and managed is paramount to survival, let alone to being successful.

The best organizations in the world not only embrace and foster a change culture (*We used to call it continuous improvement*), but try to gain market share by leading or creating change in their respective markets and industries through innovation in their products, services, or practices. The evolutionary theory author, Charles Darwin, said it with eloquence, "It is not the strongest species that survive, nor the most intelligent, but the ones most responsive to change".

The value of teamwork has now been elevated to the mission-critical status, as the complexity of global and organizational issues now demand cross-functional cooperation. Organizations can no longer simply give lip service to teamwork. The days of the star CEOs are over, and the CEO of the Year awards should be too! The credit for the win goes to team, and not its leader, coach, or captain.

The appropriate equilibrium between horizontal and vertical teamwork supports the balanced perspective between what is important to the team which an individual leads versus the team they are a member of. The proverbial silo culture comes from strong vertical teamwork and focus at the expense of other functions. The silos never disappear, as the functions are vertical, but the thickness and composition of the silo walls is what is determined. The walls are either made of reinforced titanium-encased concrete or a light meshed carbon material.

In this globally competitive world, where organizations compete fiercely for customers and talent, I would venture to say that it would be ill-advised, if not fatal, for any organization not to include the customer and respect for people & diversity on their cultural or value statement.

WELL-ENGINEERED ORGANIZATION (STRUCTURE, ROLES, & PROCESSES)

The organization is a complex technology-supported system of business processes and projects, which are often interdependent, on which is overlaid a structure of teams and roles performed by competent incumbents. Like any other system, be it the human anatomy, the space shuttle, or an ERP software, how could we predict its effectiveness, how could we repair or enhance it, or how could we predict under which environmental conditions it would fail without a blueprint? We simply cannot.

In order for the system to work, each step of each process and project has to be performed by the incumbent of only one specific role, thus ensuring that the step is executed without the conflict or turf war resulting from an overlap, or the risk of omission or ball dropping as a result of colleagues who share in the accountability and wrongfully assuming the other is carrying out the task (*I don't believe in shared accountability for that reason*). Failure to assign the appropriate authority and resources to the individual is really tantamount to the person not being accountable, as they could not effectively fulfil the accountability.

The organization's decision-making platforms or forums are where issues and options are debated and scrubbed and where the most critical decisions are made. By default, each team leader has their regular series of team meetings, with their frequency and duration designed based on the topics to be debated: operational, tactical, and strategic. The organization's leadership team, led by the Chief Executive, or leadership teams of business units and/or divisions are where strategic cross-functional business decisions are debated and ultimately made by their respective team leader because of their inherent cross-functional membership.

There are several other forums that need to exist in order to deal with other cross-functional topics of importance, such as product development, business technology, capital investment, business development, and enterprise-level projects. The existence of these forums, their charters, mandates, and memberships need to be treated as an integral part of the governance structure. In publicly-traded organizations, the Board of Directors meetings, including its committees, are the utmost decision-making forums, and their agendas and schedules also need to be integrated to the other forums. The agenda items for Board approval need to be debated first by the respective functional teams and then the executive leadership team.

If it is true that an organization is made up of a woven array of vertical and horizontal teams, then it is not only important that each team member's role be clearly defined, but that other team members be well aware of each other's roles. The accessibility of each role profile to the entire organization is also critical, as it supports the access to knowledge, and provides career visibility and a development path to those aspiring to become the incumbent of any other role.

INCUMBENTS WITH GREAT POTENTIAL WHO FIT THEIR ROLE

In an ideal world, each role in the organization is filled with an incumbent who has all of the required elements necessary to perform the role naturally, or at the reflex level. The trade off comes with either the availability of resources, or the assignment of individuals in so-called developmental roles, which by definition are designed for the individual to acquire or develop competencies that they do not currently have. In that case, a proportion of the individual's energy is expended in either fitting in or learning the role, as opposed to performing it. The cost of colleagues and team members supporting the individual's development effort, and resulting sub-optimal business performance must be worth the developmental investment (*I vividly recall when a new CEO who had prematurely been promoted was assigned to* the organization and caused a massive disruption to the business unit by applying his own ill-informed version of leadership, and proceeded with shuffling half of the executive in different roles, hence self-legitimizing the concept of 'developmental assignment'. The only things missing were the music and chairs. He nearly destroyed the organization).

Whatever you do, have people on your team who have the potential and interest to advance to the next role. They will inevitably find ways to make the processes and projects for which they are accountable better and faster, and will look for potential incumbents who can take over, and let them move on to the next big role. They are also immune to becoming obsolete if the demands of the role suddenly become greater than originally anticipated. They have performance capability and elasticity.

Those high potentials are like thoroughbreds. They are demanding, are anxious to get going, and are easily spooked by bad leaders or bad companies. The good news is, if you can have a team leader who can handle them and get them all to pull the chariot in the same direction, you will win the race. High potentials without great leadership will rapidly tear any team apart, and go nowhere fast.

GREAT PERSONAL & LEVEL-5 TEAM LEADERS

If all an organization would do is recruit and employ great leaders, I would propose that most other aspects of organizational effectiveness and performance would quite rapidly be taken care of. That's what great leaders do. The ability to identify, retain, develop, and attract great leaders is a strategic competency and a game changer.

Those great Level-5 leaders combine deep personal humility with intense professional will. They do not need to be charismatic, and should not be flamboyant. These leaders need to have a personal interest in the development and engagement of their team members, particularly with the shift in the current demographics and resulting generational mix.

It is actually true that the success of any organization starts at the top, but that is not where it ends. It ends with great teammates and leaders working well together in exceeding customer expectations. The leader at the top has all of the authority and resources they need to leverage the organization's capabilities and culture, or discard either in an autocratic or narcissistic fashion.

Upon the arrival of a new leader, the departure of team members is often triggered by a remodelling, flattening, or leaning of the structure, or as a result of a conflict of culture or strategic direction. The turnover may be necessary or understandable if intended, but it is inevitably very costly and disruptive, and tends to ripple down into the organization, as the newly appointed team members begin to do the same to their respective vertical teams. The worst-case scenario is the inadvertent selection of a counter-cultural leader with a saviour syndrome, where the impact of disruption is neither warranted, nor purposeful (*I can't believe how casual and cavalier some Boards of Directors can be when selecting senior leaders, and how trusting of recruitment firms they are*).

Too often, leaders are selected based on their track record, either as described on their resume, or as media fables and legends depict them. The tragedy of it is that, too often, which alma mater they belong too is disproportionately impactful on the decision to hire. In their 2006 book *Snakes in Suits: When Psychopaths Go to Work*[32], Paul Babiak and Robert Hare state that psychopaths fear specificity and verification of resumes and employment applications. They fear concrete and specific performance vetting in interviews, and tangible reviews of work, and concrete assessments of actual output produced. They are disproportionately represented in management, politics, media, academia, and religion. This is because their defining proclivities and talents are often masked or disguised as the stuff or defining qualities and traits of leadership, command presence, charisma, and take-charge management.

Warren Buffett summarized the thought this way, "Somebody once said that in looking for people to hire, you look for three qualities: integrity, intelligence, and energy. But if they don't have the first, the other two will kill you". Psychopaths typically resent, envy, and try to extinguish in their subordinates, those traits and capabilities they themselves do not possess whether intellectual or emotional (*Yeah...I sure can think of a few of them I either worked for, or with*).

EMOTIONALLY-ENGAGED TEAM MEMBERS

The term emotion has often been a pejorative one in business, associated with gut feeling decision-making. The idea of getting emotional when discussing issues or projects was frowned upon as a risky and irrational behaviour which would blur the real data and facts required to make sensible decisions. Business was about numbers, financials, and market share and not feelings or emotions. Worse yet, we should not talk of needs, and its most famous proponent,

Abraham Maslow, whose pyramid (Figure 72) we all heard about at one point or another (*Kind of weird that a pyramid would be the foundation, isn't it?*).

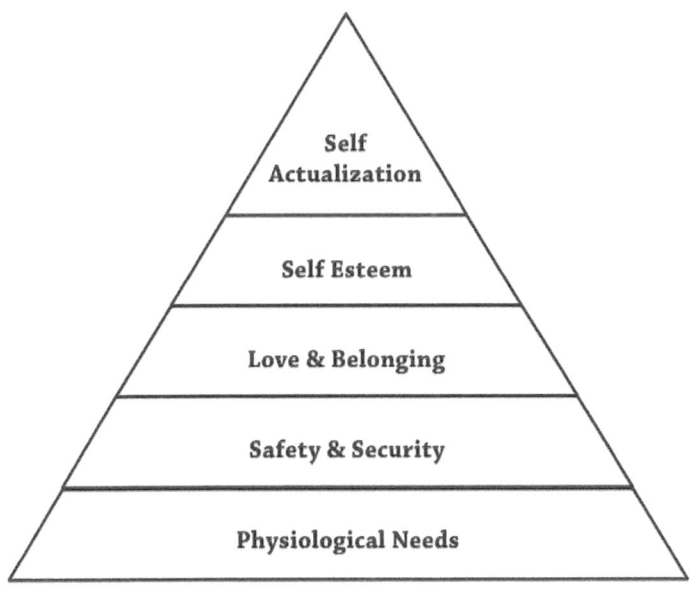

FIGURE 72 — MASLOW'S HIERARCHY OF NEEDS

The engagement concept has its roots in studies of morale or a team's willingness to accomplish goals, which really began in the 1920s. US Army researchers during WWII would attempt to measure unity of effort and attitudinal battle-readiness as a predictor of combat effectiveness. With the advent of the knowledge worker and emphasis on individual talent management, the term engagement was born. While morale is an assessment of the team's readiness, engagement relates instead to the individual team member.

In researching material for this topic, I found that the dictionary and various author definitions for employee engagement all had key elements, but none of them comprised the holistic notion. The Conference Board researched the definitions and came up with a very solid composite definition. It reads like this: 'Employee engagement is a heightened emotional and intellectual connection that an employee has for their job, organization, manager, or co-workers that, in turn, influences them to apply additional discretionary effort to their work.'

The 2012 edition of Towers Watson's Global Workforce Study best summarizes what are the key drivers of sustainable employee engagement (Figure 73).

Priority areas of focus	Behaviours and actions that matter to employees
Leadership	• Is effective at growing the business • Shows sincere interest in employees' well-being • Behaves consistently with the organization's core values • Earns employees' trust and confidence
Stress, balance and workload	• Manageable stress levels at work • A healthy balance between work and personal life • Enough employees in the group to do the job right • Flexible work arrangements
Goals and objectives	Employees understand: • The organization's business goals • Steps they need to take to reach those goals • How their job contributes to achieving goals
Supervisors	• Assign tasks suited to employees' skills • Act in ways consistent with their words • Coach employees to improve performance • Treat employees with respect

Priority areas of focus	Behaviours and actions that matter to employees
Organization's image	• Highly regarded by the general public • Displays honesty and integrity in business activities

FIGURE 73 — TOP FIVE SUSTAINABLE ENGAGEMENT DRIVERS

I learned from my kid brother—a professional baseball athlete and Olympian, that winning is impossible without emotional engagement (*Here we go with the sports analogy again...I know, but they work!*). We have all seen what happens to sports teams when the players coast around or behave like overpaid spoiled brats, without the energy, resolve, and determination needed to win. We would say that they don't care about winning or losing, that they don't want it badly enough. Caring is an emotion.

My brother says that the will to win has to be fuelled by the energy created by emotions. It was during one of my son's hockey games, in some ungodly cold arena, too early on a winter Saturday morning, when he explained that the necessary emotional component is why millionaire athletes will laugh, cry, hug and jump in each other's arms when scoring. And they do so without concern for the perception of tens of millions of spectators watching (*No worries...I am not suggesting that we need to go to that extent in business, but celebrating is certainly a parallel*). This is called emotional engagement.

There has been ample research conducted over the past decades by leading consulting and academic organizations that demonstrates the dramatic impact which engagement has on the performance of not only one team, but the aggregate of all teams, which is the organization itself. It unequivocally translates into substantially more favourable indicators, from profitability to customer satisfaction/engagement to colleague retention.

In its 2005 Global Workforce Study, Towers Perrin reported that, when asked, 72 percent of highly engaged employees believed they could positively affect customer service. They also found that the organization's focus on customer satisfaction was in the top 10 list of engagement drivers. The 2012 version of the same study by Towers Watson showed that, for a sample of 50 global companies, those with high sustainable engagement posted an average one-year operating margin close to three times higher than those with low employee engagement, at just over 27 percent. A customer-focused organization supports highly engaged colleagues, who drive customer satisfaction and financial performance, which in turn creates shareholder value (*You reach the logical conclusion...employee engagement is a leading indicator of both customer satisfaction and shareholder value*).

Another 12-month study of 50 multinational companies, published in 2009 by the same global HR consultancy, showed an astonishing relationship between engagement and performance: highly engaged workforces posted a 19.2 percent increase in operating income, while those with low engagement scores saw their operating income drop by 32.7 percent. (*If that is not hard-wiring the soft engagement stuff to business results, what is?*). The same study showed a direct correlation between employee engagement and customer satisfaction (*Satisfied customers don't create engagement. It's the other way around*).

VERTICALLY & HORIZONTALLY ALIGNED STRATEGY-EXECUTION PERFORMANCE GOALS

The sharing of strategic goals within each function, and also across functions, is designed to ensure the vertical and horizontal alignment of these objectives. We discussed earlier the need for teammates to understand each other's role. While the roles themselves tend to be relatively static, the annual objectives change every year and need to be assigned and understood within each team. The awareness of these objectives and related initiatives is important to other functions, or horizontal team members, either because of their potential impact on their function or the opportunity they present to partner and contribute to their achievement. The use of business technology makes the process of communicating these objectives easier.

KEY PERFORMANCE INDICATORS (KPIs), SCORECARD, & BENCHMARKS

There cannot be performance assessment, or improvements for that matter, without knowing what the performance indicators will show when we are succeeding or making progress against the targets that we have set for ourselves (*It's good to stay on track, as long as we move forward so that the train does not run us over*). But, even if we are doing well by our standards, how can we know which league we are playing in without benchmarking our own organization's metrics against our peers in our league—or in the league we aspire to play in? Not only do we have to pick the leading or predictive and lagging or trailing indicators that measure our progress, success, and performance, but we need to know which ones the league uses so we can gauge ourselves. The aggregate or balanced view of those indicators is what matters as opposed to any single one of those indicators.

PEOPLE AND TEAMS ARE REWARDED AND RECOGNIZED FOR DISCIPLINED EXECUTION

When it comes to rewarding disciplined execution, organizations must be prepared to put their money where their mouth is. They cannot simply reward individual achievement when success is inconceivable without teamwork and team performance. The compensation program needs to reward both levels of contribution. What is rewarded is the disciplined execution of what was committed to, and in a way that lives and respects the organization's core values.

OPEN TWO-WAY COMMUNICATION & CONSULTATION

The open and candid communication amongst colleagues, both with their team leader and throughout the organization, means that the real and truthful issues, opportunities, and obstacles are communicated, discussed, and debated. This enables rapid and sound decision making by exploring solutions at the full width of the possibility spectrum.

Candid:	Marked by honest sincere expression. Indicating or suggesting sincere honesty and absence of deception. Expressing opinions and feelings in an honest and sincere way

I learned a long time ago as a military information officer that creating great expectations, and then unexpectedly failing to deliver on them, is one of the best ways to destroy the morale and combat effectiveness or engagement of troops. We witnessed it during WWII when the Allied propaganda machine would impersonate Nazis and proclaim battle wins against the Allies over the German airwaves, only to retract the good news later on. It is therefore not wise to sugar coat information, speculate or create unrealistic expectations (*Remember, the truth is always harder to sell*).

The consulting of colleagues is simply acknowledging that they too are owners of the organization, and deserve the respect of being consulted about their respective areas of accountability and on matters that impact their work life within the organization. Not to do so is disingenuous and conducive to disengagement.

CONCLUSION—SO WHAT DOES ALL OF THIS MEAN?

When all is said and done, what matters to organizations is that they perform optimally at any point and time, and by optimal, we mean to the best of our ability. Striving to be better than our competitors and doing that, over time, requires an adaptive quality to continue to be successful in an environment which is changing at an exponentially increasing rate. The only way to know is to have the right control panel or dashboard, combined with the right benchmarks.

Organizations are made up of people who either lead a team, are a member of one, or who are both. Performance is about having great people who are emotionally engaged, and working very well together in getting things done. The things they get done are business processes and projects, and the special objectives they must meet to support the achievement of a business plan and strategy. The clarity of the goals, the clarity of their role, and the vertical and horizontal alignment of their respective contribution are key to not wasting precious performance energy. They execute the plan in a systematic and disciplined way.

Their engagement is a function of only a few well-understood key factors. The first and foremost of which is the quality of the organization's team leaders. Quality leaders understand the turbo-like power of emotions, and recognize that values and beliefs are fundamentally an emotional phenomenon, which is a source of greatness if properly aligned, and causes enduring conflicts if misaligned. People are about relationships, and relationships are about interpersonal communication. Great organizations and people are masters at communication at all levels; between individuals, teams, and at the organization/institution level. They know that communication is about clarity, truth, relevance, and recency.

The equation for organizational high-performance only has a few key fundamental variables which we pretty well all know by now (*Unless we have been frozen in time*). It starts with a great Level-5 leader at the top who will put together a great team of humble, determined, and passionate leaders who in turn will do the same (*Or will graciously exit the wrong players*). These individuals are passionate about what they do, who they do it for, and who they do it with.

The person on that top team who is accountable for people and organizational effectiveness and development (*We call them CHROs*) will be the generator, custodian, and auditor (*And often the apostle*) of the organizational, team, and individual approaches to solve that equation. Needless to say, they will not do that on their own, but only in complicity with a great team (*I know that for a fact. Been there. Done that. Have a dresser full of T-shirts*). That equation is a simple one to solve, so beware of those who, out of self-interest or preservation, will try to make you feel panicked or inadequate by making it so complex (*Especially consultants*).

Organizations, teams, and even individuals are easy to understand and predict if you pay attention long enough, providing you have the courage to accept the science and fundamental evidence of how people interact when they try to get things done. There are great, simple models out there that are supported by solid research. Like a scientist in a laboratory using mice and monkeys to test their assumptions, organizational scientists observe high-performance teams and people in their natural organizational habitat and are careful not to underestimate the power of simple analogies.

Team players will compare themselves to the teams that they understand and follow, be they professional sporting teams or the crews manning glamorous systems like aircraft and space shuttles. Some of them learned the value of teamwork by playing music in a band, many from playing team sports at an early age.

Most of the world's top-performing organizations essentially do it the same way and use the same performance model (Figure 74). They don't adopt the latest theory and zigzag their way into greatness—most new theories end up being flawed to some extent—instead they continue with the proven recipe until a better one is tried and tested. Top-performing organizations know when to hit the reset button and reboot an unwieldy complex program. They know when to unwrap themselves from around the axle and go back to basics. They don't dwell on how successful they feel they have been. They know it for a fact because they measure and compare, and they strive to be even more successful by tomorrow.

FIGURE 74 — HIGH-PERFORMANCE EQUATION MODEL

The frighteningly simple fact is that great organizations are engineered in a way to systematically adapt to dynamic change; they understand the variables and constants in the high-performance equation and constantly keep solving the equation. They know that the two most important elements of the equation are leadership and teamwork. They never compromise either. This is not rocket science.

EPILOGUE

It took me longer than I expected to write this book. I had more to say than I thought, and it was difficult at times to structure what I believe in and what I learned into a natural and coherent flow. If it hadn't been for my wife's lovingly supportive encouragement and vigilance, and the fact that too many people I respect knew that I was writing it, this book would probably still be a partial manuscript, and I would have sentenced myself to that awful feeling that comes with procrastination.

I have had many second thoughts about publishing it: Perhaps nobody will buy it, and maybe it's presumptuous and arrogant of me to think I know enough about this subject to write a book, and worse yet, what if some people buy the book, read it, and think it was a waste of their reading time and their money? I finally realized that the reason I wanted to write it in the first place was to help people be successful at what I irreverently call the performance thing, by sharing what I have learned from people who took the time to show me.

I tried to make the book informative and stayed away from turning it into a textbook (*Not that I would be academically qualified enough to even contemplate doing that*) and caught myself having to share what was in the back of my mind while I was writing it. I hope I was not too candid with my *'color commentary'* and that I did not distract you by doing so, or failed at being a bit humorous. I just can't help but laugh at some of the too-often blatant irony behind the counter-productive people practices of poorly-performing organizations (*That is why I love to read Dilbert® cartoons and I am a big fan of Catbert® the evil HR Director*).

There is a big difference between being serious about work, and taking yourself and organizational life too seriously. The best people and leaders I know laugh a lot and are having fun doing what they do. I made my sons and many colleagues listen to 'The sunscreen song' by Baz Luhrmann; it's a great life theme song. When work and the organization (*Or the outfit*) is getting to you, and in the way of enjoying life, remember that this is only a job and that there are more important things in life to worry about, such as health, family, and friendships.

I don't know what is next for me after publishing this book. Maybe I'll write another book, maybe I'll try my hand at teaching or consulting, or maybe I'll head back to the corporate world as an HR guy. If you enjoyed the book, and I sure as heck hope you did, maybe I will write another one. I am looking forward to hearing from you, either way. Take care.

ACKNOWLEDGEMENTS

I am thankful to the following individuals for their support and friendship, but most importantly for their candid feedback and suggestions in making the original manuscript far better than it would have been otherwise: My son William, my father Jean-Paul, my brother Alain, my friend Peter Vokey, and my former colleagues and teammates; Stéphanie Boucher, Gail Conway, Teal Backus and Brock McCarthy.

I would have never had the self-motivation or determination to start this book, let alone finish it, without the love, counsel, patience, and encouragement of my wife and best friend Trinda. I used to suspect that she could be an extraordinary HR advisor, for having listened to my countless episodes of ranting, raving, and wondering about crazy jobs and people issues over the past 30 years. Now I know that she actually is.

ABOUT THE AUTHOR

Mario G. Patenaude prides himself in being branded as a passionate business-driven Human Resources leader. He not only understands and believes in, but also has experienced, the performance impact of a simple, systematic, and integrated HR program driven by a high-performance HR team and actively supported by great business leaders.

As a senior HR and Communications executive, he has successfully played a leadership role in setting and delivering the mergers and acquisitions, transformational and growth agenda for private, start-up, publicly-traded and family-owned corporations as well as public-service organizations. He is also recognized as an authority in the field of HR transformation. He has worked on most continents for admired high-performance organizations in the technology, communication, life sciences, aerospace, defense, consumer package goods, and professional services sectors. He has held consulting and thought-leadership roles in the fields of career, leadership, and team development for marquee professional services firms.

He gives credit to the great teams he has led, his executive leadership team colleagues, and the many world-class consultants, who courageously provided him with the guidance and subject-matter expertise, for allowing him to be part of such success stories.

Mario is a business graduate of Université de Montréal's École des Hautes Études Commerciales (HEC), the United States Defense Information School (DINFOS), and of the Harvard Business School Executive Education Program, and holds a Certified Human Resources Professional (CHRP) designation. He is the President of Integral Human Resources Management Consulting, which he founded in 1997. For more information on Mario, to learn about his next book, or to seek his advice please see his website at www.integralhr.ca.

BIBLIOGRAPHY

ENDNOTES

1. Barker, Joel A. The Power of Vision. [Video] Star Thrower, 1990.
2. Seligman, Martin. Authentic Happiness. New York, NY: Free Press, 2002.
3. Collins, James. Built To Last: Successful Habits Of Visionary Companies. New York, NY: Harper Business, 1994.
4. Lencioni, Patrick. Death By Meeting: A Leadership Fable-- About Solving The Most Painful Problem In Business. San Francisco, CA: Jossey-Bass, 2004.
5. Hammer, Michael. Reengineering The Corporation: A Manifesto For Business Revolution. New York, NY: Harper Business Essentials, 2003.
6. Tuckman, Bruce, et al. Stages in Small Group Development Revisited. ABI/INFORM Global, 1977.
7. Katzenbach, Jon. The Wisdom Of Teams: Creating The High-Performance Organization. Boston, MA: Harvard Business School Press, 1993.
8. Wageman, Ruth, et al. Senior Leadership Teams: What It Takes To Make Them Great. Boston, MA: Harvard Business School Press, 2008.

9. Lencioni, Patrick. The Five Dysfunctions Of A Team: A Leadership Fable. San Francisco, CA: Jossey-Bass, 2002.
10. de Bono, Edward. Six Thinking Hats. Boston, MA: Little, Brown, 1985.
11. Daughtry, Timothy, and Casselman, Gary. Executing Strategy: From Boardroom to Frontline. Sterling, VA: Capital Books Inc., 2009.
12. Jaques, Elliot. Requisite Organisation: A Total System for Effective Managerial Organisation and Managerial Leadership for the Twenty-first Century. Arlington VA: Cason Hall & Co., 1989.
13. McClelland, D.C. "Testing For Competence Rather That For Intelligence." American Psychologist. 1973: 28, 1-14
14. Boyatzis, Richard. The Competent Manager: A Model For Effective Performance. New York, NY: Wiley, 1982.
15. Collins, James. Good To Great: Why Some Companies Make The Leap—And Others Don't. New York, NY: Harper Business, 2001.
16. Greenleaf, Robert K. "The Servant as Leader." Indianapolis, IN: Greenleaf Center for Servant Leadership, 1970.
17. Hersey, Paul, and Blanchard, Ken. Management Of Organizational Behavior: Utilizing Human Resources. Englewood Cliffs, NJ: Prentice-Hall, 1972.
18. Goleman, Daniel. Primal Leadership: Realizing The Power Of Emotional Intelligence. Boston, MA: Harvard Business School Press, 2002.

19. Bass, Bernard. Improving Organizational Effectiveness Through Transformational Leadership. Thousand Oaks, CA: Sage Publications, 1994.
20. Ulrich, David. The Leadership Code: Five Rules To Lead By. Boston, MA: Harvard Business Press, 2008.
21. Covey, Stephen. The Seven Habits Of Highly Effective People: Restoring The Character Ethic. New York, NY: Simon and Schuster, 1989.
22. Gladwell, Malcolm. Outliers: The Story Of Success. New York, NY: Little, Brown and Co, 2008.
23. Hankin, Steven. The War For Talent. Chicago. IL: McKinsey & Company, 1997
24. Ambler, Tim, and Barrow, Simon. "The Employer Brand." Journal of Brand Management, 1996: 4, 185-206
25. Watkins, Michael. The First 90 Days: Critical Success Strategies For New Leaders At All Levels. Boston, MA: Harvard Business School Press, 2003.
26. Kotter, John. Leading Change. Boston, MA: Harvard Business School Press, 1996.
27. Friedman, Thomas. The World Is Flat: A Brief History Of The Twenty-First Century. New York, NY: Farrar, Straus and Giroux, 2005.
28. Kaplan, Robert. The Balanced Scorecard: Translating Strategy Into Action. Boston, MA: Harvard Business School Press, 1996.
29. Fornell, Claes, et al."Customer Satisfaction and Stock Prices: High Returns, Low Risk." Journal of Marketing January 2006.
30. Wang, Feifei, et al. "Association of Healthcare Costs with Per Unit Body Mass Index Increase."

Journal of Occupational & Environmental Medicine July 2006.
31. Alboher, Marci. One Person/Multiple Careers: A New Model For Work/Life Success. New York, NY: Warner Business Books, 2007.
32. Babiak, Paul. Snakes In Suits: When Psychopaths Go To Work. New York, NY: Regan Books, 2006.

www.ingramcontent.com/pod-product-compliance
Lightning Source LLC
Chambersburg PA
CBHW020636220526
45464CB00001B/165